G C S E

English

SPELLING
and VOCABULARY

Margaret Hyder
Catherine Hilton

EDUCATIONAL

Every effort has been made to trace copyright holders and to obtain their permission for the use of copyright material. The author and publishers will gladly receive information enabling them to rectify any error or omission in subsequent editions.

First published 1997

Letts Educational
Aldine House
Aldine Place
London W12 8AW
Telephone: 0181 740 2266

Text: ©MCH 1997

Design and illustrations ©BPP (Letts Educational) Ltd 1997

Design, page layout and illustrations: Moondisks Ltd, Cambridge

British Library Cataloguing-in-Publication Data

A CIP record for this book is available from the British Library

ISBN 1 85758 655 7

Printed and bound in Great Britain by Sterling Press

Letts Educational is the trading name of BPP (Letts Educational) Ltd

Contents

Introduction

Spelling

This section is divided into two parts.

Part 1 Techniques This explains the various techniques you can use when learning the spelling of words.

Part 2 Rules and Patterns The most useful rules and patterns are given together with advice on how to learn any exceptions to the rules. In addition, you are given guidance on words that are commonly confused.

In order to familiarise yourself with all the techniques, we suggest you work systematically through Part 1. You can then select from Part 2 the rules and patterns you need to learn.

In most chapters, under the heading **_For you to do_** there is an activity for you to undertake. This will enable you to work actively at improving your spelling and will also provide you with a greater understanding of a particular technique, rule or pattern.

Vocabulary

This section of the book provides you with advice about improving your vocabulary and presents you with a variety of words to use for specific situations.

You can work systematically through the chapters in this section or you can select individual chapters to meet your needs.

Don't attempt to work through all the chapters in one go. We recommend you study one chapter at a time. Certainly don't tackle Chapters 19, 20 and 21 together as you won't be able to remember all the new vocabulary you are introduced to.

At times we ask you to carry out certain activities under the heading **_For you to do_**. Enlarging your vocabulary is an active pursuit and the activities help you to use and remember words. You will need a dictionary and thesaurus to refer to as you work through this section.

Consultant Editor

The consultant editor for this book is Ian Barr. Ian has years of experience teaching English and is a GCSE Chief Examiner.

section 1
spelling

Chapter 1 **Introducing Spelling**

What can you do to improve your spelling?

■ Be confident about spelling.

Don't: avoid using a word because you are uncertain about its spelling

stop to look up the spelling of a word in a dictionary while you are writing.

Do: spell the word as you think and then check it after you've finished writing.

■ Choose your target words to learn.
Your target words might be:

words you often want to use but don't know how to spell

difficult words that you need for the subjects you are studying

words that you have difficulty spelling. These may be identified by you or your tutor.

You will add new words to this list of target words as you become more aware of your spelling needs.

■ Practise learning your target words.
You need to:

practise just a few target words at a time

keep practising these words over several days.

■ Use techniques and approaches when you learn spellings.
These techniques and approaches may be:

visual (see Chapter 2)

taking words apart (see Chapter 3)

adapting the pronunciation (see Chapter 4)

memory aids (see Chapter 5)

using a dictionary (see Chapter 6)

'rules' (see Chapters 7–12)

Remember:
you will need to use different techniques for different words
sometimes you will need to combine techniques.

■ Proof-read your writing.
  You will need to:
      check your first and final drafts
      underline any words you are uncertain about
      use a dictionary to check these spellings
      use the computer's spell-check if you are using a computer.

Remember:
Computer spell-checks won't always help. Some have American spellings listed. On other occasions, you may have made the wrong choice, e.g. **their** for **there**, and the computer won't show this as a mistake.

| Why is spelling important? |

Correct spelling:
■ shows you care about your writing
■ helps your reader to understand what you have written
■ gives your reader confidence in your writing and your ideas
■ shows that you know and can follow spelling conventions.

Checkpoints
■ Correct spelling is important – it can help you to gain marks in exams.
■ You can improve your spelling if you want to.
■ Keep a list of the words you need to learn, and work on a few at a time.
■ Follow the advice we give you in this chapter and the information about techniques, rules and patterns in the following chapters.

Chapter 2 Looking at Words

What is the visual technique?

■ The visual technique enables you to learn the spelling of a word by remembering the way it looks.

The visual technique

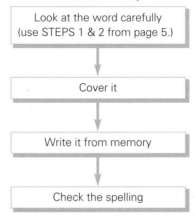

Look at the word carefully
(use STEPS 1 & 2 from page 5.)

↓

Cover it

↓

Write it from memory

↓

Check the spelling

■ You will need to use this technique on a word several times before you remember the spelling and are able to write the word correctly every time.

■ You are most likely to be successful if you practise over several days.

Why is the visual technique important?

■ Spelling is mainly a visual skill.

■ Good spellers automatically write words correctly. They can 'see' the correct spelling in their minds and transfer this to the page. They have a good visual memory.

■ Not everyone has this skill but it can be developed. (See the section **How to improve your visual memory** on page 5.)

■ This technique is especially useful for words with a distinctive shape or pattern.

■ It can help you learn difficult irregular words.

Examples: gauge   analysis   awkward

| How to improve your visual memory |

- Become more aware of words and what they look like.
- Look carefully at words and practise visualising them:

> STEP 1: *Look at the overall shape of the word. (The word will need to be written in lower case letters, i.e. not capitals.)*
> Example: fascinate

> STEP 2: *Look for special features and problem parts*
> Example: fa**sc**inate
>
> (Concentrate on the **sc** letter combination.)

For you to do

Look at your list of target words. Choose any words you think would be best learnt by the visual technique. Use this technique to learn the spelling of each of these words.

Proof-reading

- By being aware of the look of words, you will increase your chances of seeing which words you have spelt incorrectly.
- You will also be more aware of possible and probable letter combinations and so make better guesses about the spelling of words.
- When you are proof-reading a piece of written work:
  - if you are uncertain about the spelling of a word you have written, try writing it out in various ways to see which looks right
  - choose the spelling that looks correct and check that spelling in a dictionary.

Checkpoints

- Using the visual technique is probably the most effective way of improving your spelling.
- Any word can be learnt using the visual technique.

Chapter 3 **Taking Words Apart**

Taking a word apart usually means that you divide it into syllables.

What is a syllable?

■ This is the definition of a syllable in *Chambers Concise Dictionary*

> **syllable** sil'a-bl, *n.* a word or part of a
> word uttered by a single effort of the voice.

In the *Glossary* we define a syllable as 'a word or part of a word that can be made by one effort of breath'.

■ Words with one syllable include:

    ache   strength   force

■ In these two-syllable words the oblique (/) shows the split between the two syllables:

    nev / er   af / fect   chap / ter
    hus / band   ceil / ing   so / cial

■ These words have three or more syllables:

    con / tin / ent (3)   dis / or / der / ly (4)
    in / se / cur / it / y (5)   com / pu / ter / i / sa / tion (6)

Why is this technique useful?

Dividing words into syllables:
■ makes long words less daunting to spell
■ allows you to break a long, difficult word into more manageable units
■ stops you missing out a syllable from a long word
■ enables you to concentrate on one part of a word at a time and learn its pattern
■ helps you with words you are not accustomed to spelling – you can split them into shorter and more manageable parts
■ encourages you to look more carefully at words and be more aware of the letter patterns within words.

How to divide a word into syllables

If the idea of syllables is new to you, then it may help if you cup your hand firmly under your chin while you are saying the following word clearly and loudly.

fantastic

You will feel your chin pressing into your hand three times, once for every syllable.

fan / tas / tic

If you practise this approach a few times within different words, you should become more aware of syllables.

The following points may also help you.

■ Just as every English word contains a vowel so does every syllable. Remember, a **y** can also act like a vowel at times.

Examples: why   *one syllable,* **y** *sounds like the vowel* **i**
hap / py   *two syllables,* **y** *sounds like the vowel* **e**

■ A syllable can also be a vowel or **y** on its own.

Examples: o / pen   ver / y

■ When you are learning the spelling of a word which contains double consonants, it is best to divide between the double consonants as it draws your attention to them. If you say the syllables as you write the word, you will hear each consonant, and this should help you to spell the word correctly.

Examples: ter / ror   ap / point   dis / con / nect

■ Although there are rules for dividing words into syllables, it is better to divide words in ways that are most helpful to you.

For you to do

Follow the advice given above and try to divide these words into syllables.

reinforce   forgotten   occupy   absolute   supervise
orbit   tomorrow   popularity   concentrated   shivering

Words within words

When you are taking words apart to learn them, you may also find it helpful to notice if a syllable forms a word in its own right.

Examples: main / ten / nance   bar / bar / ian
main   ten   bar   bar

techniques

Being able to see these syllables as words within a longer word does help to jog your memory about the spelling of the longer word.

▪ Sometimes you will see words within words that do not follow the division of the word into syllables.

Example: sincerely
             divided into syllables would be
             sin / cere / ly

but it may be easier to remember the spelling by dividing it into two words

             sincerely
             since   rely

Remember, always divide a word up in the way that is most helpful to you.

Compound words

Separate words are sometimes put together in English to form a longer word. You may find it helpful when spelling if you can spot the separate words within the longer word.

Examples: underage   downward   cupboard
             under+age   down+ward   cup+board

Combining techniques

▪ If after you have taken a word apart you have difficulty remembering the spelling of any of the parts, try using the visual technique shown in Chapter 2 to help you learn that part.

▪ In the next chapter you will be shown how you can adapt the way you pronounce syllables and parts of words to help you remember the spelling of difficult, irregular words.

Checkpoints

▪ By taking words apart to learn them, you will find you only have to focus on a small part at a time rather than on the whole word.

▪ This technique is particularly helpful for long, regular words; words which have double consonants; and when you are trying to spell an unfamiliar word.

Chapter 4 **Adapting the Pronunciation**

What is this technique?

▨ This approach builds on the technique shown in Chapter 3 *Taking Words Apart.*

▨ Some words are spelt as they are pronounced. These are regular words. As you saw in Chapter 3, when you want to learn the spelling of a long, regular word, you can:

◗ divide the word into syllables

◗ listen to the sound made by each syllable

◗ spell out each syllable in turn.

▨ Other words are not spelt as they are pronounced. When you are learning the spelling of such words you can:

◗ divide the word into syllables

◗ change the way you say a syllable to fit the way it is spelt.

Examples:	despair	**des** / pair	say **des** for the first syllable
	particular	par / tic / u / **lar**	stress **lar** for the last syllable
	listen	lis / **ten**	say **ten** at the end

Why is this technique useful?

▨ This approach is simple to use and is one that most students find easy.

▨ It help you to spell irregular words.

▨ It draws your attention to missing letters or parts of words.

▨ It reminds you about unclear or indistinct-sounding letters or parts within words.

techniques

| How to use this technique |

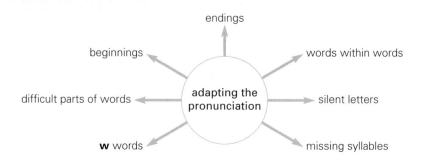

endings

beginnings

words within words

difficult parts of words

adapting the pronunciation

silent letters

w words

missing syllables

Beginnings

▨ In English we often stress the first syllable of a word. This makes the beginning easy to hear and quite clear.

▨ If the stress does not fall on the beginning of a word, the sound of the first letters may be unclear. This can make it difficult for you to decide how to spell the word.

▨ To help you remember the spelling, try adapting the pronunciation by stressing the first part.

Examples: **de**cision   **pre**cise
             protrude   **des**cription

Endings

▨ When the stress is on the first part of a word, your voice trails off at the end of it. Therefore the ending of a word is often difficult to spell because you cannot hear the sound properly.

▨ If you stress the pronunciation of the end of such words as you learn them, spelling them becomes easier.

▨ You will not need to use this technique as much when you become used to certain patterns appearing at the ends of words. (You can always learn words with the same ending as a group. See Chapter 5 *Memory Aids*.)

For each of the endings below, read the words in the list aloud and pronounce the ending as it is spelt.

-ar	-ary	-age
peculiar	contemporary	passage
spectacular	secondary	image
grammar	temporary	garage
similar	dictionary	village

-ant	-ice	-ent
relevant	notice	permanent
ignorant	crevice	different
fragrant	malice	independent
extravagant	police	impudent

Missing syllables

■ Some words are misspelt because part of the word, or a letter in it, appears to be missing.

Examples: in / **ter** / est / ing   *the **e** in **ter** is sometimes missed out*
es / **tu** / ary   *the middle syllable disappears as we say the word*
gen / **er** / al   *the **e** in **er** is sometimes missed out*

■ As you write the word, say each syllable slowly and carefully, stressing the difficult syllable. This will stop you missing out letters.

Words within words

■ If you can see a word within another word and stress the pronunciation of that shorter word, it will help you to spell tricky words.

Examples: theory   **the** / **or** / y

You can see the words **the** and **or** in **theory** but when you say the word **theory** you can't hear **the** and **or**.
Try adapting the way you say **theory** so you can hear the words **the** and **or**.
Other examples include:

character   char / **act** / er
nuclear   nu / **clear**
early   **ear** / ly
friend   fri / **end**
courteous   **court** / e / ous

Difficult parts of words

▨ Treat the problem part as if it were a word within the longer word.

▨ Isolate that part and adapt the way you say it.

Examples: chocolate   choc / **o** / late   *Stress the **o***
   convenient   con / **ven** / ient   *Stress the **ven***
   enemy   en / **e** / my   *Stress the second **e***

Silent letters

▨ If you have difficulty in remembering a silent letter in a word, try pronouncing the silent letter as you write the word.

Examples: subtle   *say su**b**tle*
   budget   *stress bu**d**get*
   biscuit   *stress the **u** in bisc**u**it*
   exhibition   *stress the **h** in ex**h**ibition*

w words

▨ The letter **w** can be silent before an **r**. If you forget to spell such words with a **w**, try stressing the **w** sound at the beginning before the **r** sound.

Examples: **w**rinkle   **w**rist   **w**rangle

▨ The letter **h** when it follows a **w** can be silent. Try splitting the word between the **w** and the **h** and stressing the **h**.

Examples: w / **h**ile   w / **h**isper   w / **h**irl

▨ **w** can change the sound of the letter or letters that follow it. Try saying the words as they are spelt and not as you would normally pronounce them.

Examples: was   *say w / **as***   want   *say w / **ant***
   ward   *say w / **ard***   warm   *say w / **arm***
   worth   *say w / **orth***   worse   *say w / **orse***

Checkpoints

▨ If you have difficulty spelling a word because it is not spelt as you pronounce it, make the way you say the word fit the spelling. This will help you to remember the spelling of the word and will act as a trigger whenever you need to write that word.

techniques

Chapter 5 Memory Aids

What are memory aids?

A memory aid is a rhyme, phrase, group of words or a diagram that we use to help us remember information.

Example: Compass directions are easy to remember with this memory aid.

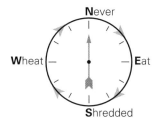

We use memory aids:
- to help us to learn and remember information
- as a 'trigger' to help us recall that information.

You may find that memory aids can help you to remember and recall difficult spelling patterns.

Examples: To remember the pattern of **c** and **s** in
ne**c**e**ss**ary
try saying '**one c**ollar and **two s**ocks'.

The **eau** part of
b**eau**tiful
can be remembered by '**e**lephants **a**re **u**gly'.

In this chapter you will be looking at various ways of helping you to remember spellings:

Grouping words together
Using phrases and sentences
Learning word 'families'
Pin-pointing the differences

techniques

Why are memory aids useful?

Memory aids are particularly useful for remembering the spelling of words:
- with difficult double letter combinations
- containing silent letters
- that are exceptions to spelling rules
- that sound alike but are spelt differently and have different meanings. (These are called homophones.)

Some useful memory aids

Grouping words together

If you group words together that share the same spelling pattern, you are more likely to:
- remember the pattern
- learn the words quickly.

Examples: **eight** **w**eight h**eight**
bru**i**se fru**i**t ru**i**n su**i**t
here **there** everyw**here**
obed**ient** conven**ient** exped**ient**

Using phrases and sentences

This technique follows on from grouping words together.
- Having grouped words together, you might find you remember them more easily if you then devise a memorable phrase or sentence for that group.

Examples: The br**ui**sed fr**ui**t r**ui**ned my s**ui**t. *ui words*

Wendy **w**riggled and **w**restled her way into her **w**rinkled **W**rangler jeans. *silent **w** words*

The wicked bandit
Who practised dec**ei**t
Gazed at the c**ei**ling
And s**ei**zed the rec**ei**pt.

This rhyme can help you to remember some **ei** words from the spelling rule for **ie** / **ei** words. See Chapter 11.
- You may also find it helpful to devise a memorable phrase or sentence for a single word that always causes you problems.

Examples: two **c**s and two **m**s in 'a**cc**o**mm**odation' two **m**s, two **t**s, two **e**s in 'co**mmittee**' *Counting out the letters helps you to remember single and double letter combinations.*

A **secret**ary can keep a **secret**. *This helps you to include the unclear part in 'secretary'.*

Learning word 'families'
 You may find that learning spellings in word families can help you to remember a pattern more quickly and easily.

Example: cancel
          cancelling
            cancelled
              cancellation

When you add -**ing**, -**ed** and -**ation** endings to **cancel**, you double the **l**. Instead of learning each word separately, remember the word family and you can learn three words at once!

Pin-pointing the differences
 Memory aids can also help you to work out which of a pair of homophones to use. Use the memory aid to pin-point the difference between the two words.

Example: stationary   stationery
                  ⇓   ⇓
             remaining still   paper, envelopes, etc.

Remember the difference in meaning and spelling by 'a station**e**ry shop sells envelop**e**s'.

For you to do
Look at your target words and see which of your words could be learnt by using some of the memory aids we have shown you.

Checkpoints
 If you have difficulty remembering a spelling pattern or rule, try using a memory aid to help you.
 You will probably find the most useful memory aids are those you devise for yourself.

Chapter 6 | Using a Dictionary

Everyone needs to use a dictionary at some time to check the spelling of a word. In this chapter you will be looking at using dictionaries as a spelling technique. In the *Vocabulary* section, Chapter 15, you will be considering the importance of using dictionaries for developing vocabulary.

What type of dictionary do you need?

- You need a dictionary that suits your needs and is easy for you to use.
- You may decide you need more than one dictionary:
  - a pocket or spelling dictionary to carry with you
  - a larger more detailed dictionary for reference at home.
- It is best to buy a 'good' dictionary produced by a leading publisher.
- Cheap 'special purchase' dictionaries rarely contain sufficient detail to be helpful, e.g. they may not show changes to spelling when endings are added.

Choosing the right dictionary

Spelling dictionaries
- These are specialist dictionaries which include more entries than other dictionaries of a similar size.
- They give simple definitions which allow you to check you have chosen the correct word.
- Spelling dictionaries show changes in spelling when endings are added.

Here is part of a page from *The Pan Spelling Dictionary*

cambium growing layer in a stem	**cancan** type of dance
cambric fine thin cloth	**cancel** to cross out; to put off
came pt. of come	*cancellation cancelled* (U.S. *canceled*)
camel animal with hump(s) used in the desert	*cancelling* (U.S. *canceling*)
camel-hair	**cancer** diseased growth in the body
camellia evergreen shrub	*cancerous*
cameo stone with a raised design	**Cancer** Crab, constellation and zodiac sign
cameos	**candelabrum** branched candlestick
camera apparatus for taking photographs	*candelabra*
cameraman	**candid** [same sound as **candied**] frank

— from *The Pan Spelling Dictionary*

Pocket dictionaries

■ These dictionaries contain fewer entries than similar-sized spelling dictionaries.

■ They provide more details about the meanings and usage of a word than a spelling dictionary, but they may not show all the changes of spelling when endings are added.

Here is an entry from *The Pocket Oxford Dictionary*. The bold **ll** on the first line shows that two **ll**s are sometimes needed when an ending is added, but the words are not listed

---

trǎ'vel. 1. *v.t.* & *t.* (ll-**ll**-). Make journey(s) esp. of some length to distant countries, traverse (country, distance) thus, (*ordered to travel for his health*; *has travelled the world*); (colloq.) withstand long journey (*wines that travel badly*); act as COMMERCIAL traveller (*for* firm, *in* commodity); (of machine or part) move *along* bar etc., *in* groove etc.); pass esp. in deliberate or systematic manner from point to point (*his eye travelled over the scene*); move, proceed, in specified manner or at specified rate (*travels at 600 m.p.h.*; *light travels faster than sound*); (colloq.) move quickly; ~**ling bag**, small bag carried by hand, for traveller's requisites; ~**ling clock**, small clock in a case; ~**ling crane** (moving on esp. overhead support); *****~**ing salesman**, commercial traveller.

— from *The Pocket Oxford Dictionary*

Concise dictionaries

■ These dictionaries contain more entries than spelling or pocket dictionaries and give more information under each entry.

■ They can be more complicated to use, but it is valuable to have one at home or in school/college as a reference source.

Here is the entry in *Chambers Concise Dictionary* for **travel**. You will notice that the spelling of **travelling**, **travelled** and **traveller** is given

---

travel *trav'l, v.i.* to journey: to go: to go round soliciting orders: to move along a course: to go with impetus: to be capable of withstanding a journey: to move.—*v.t.* to journey over or through:—*pr.p.* **trav'elling**; *pa.t.* and *pa.p.* **trav'elled.**—*n.* journeying.—*adj.* **trav'elled** having made journeys: experienced: frequented.—*n.* **trav'eller** one who travels or has travelled: one of the travelling people: one who travels for a mercantile house: a piece of mechanism that moves on a gantry, etc.—*n.* and *adj.* **trav'elling.**—*n.* **travelogue** (*trav'ə-log*) a talk, lecture, article, or film on travel.—**travel agency** an agency which provides information, brochures, tickets, etc., relating to travel; **travel agent; traveller's cheque** a cheque which can be cashed at any foreign branch or specified agent of the bank issuing it; **trav'eller's-joy** *Clematis vitalba*, sometimes called old man's beard; **travelling folk, people** the name by which itinerant people often call themselves, in preference to the derogatory names gipsies or tinkers.—*adj.* **trav'el-sick** suffering from travel sickness.—**travel sickness** nausea experienced, as a result of motion, by a passenger in a car, ship, aircraft, etc. [**travail**.]

— from *Chambers Concise Dictionary*

Phonetically arranged dictionaries

▓ These are sometimes sold as 'the poor spellers' dictionaries' as entries for both regular and irregular words are spelt as they are pronounced. (See Chapter 4 *Adapting the Pronunciation*.)

▓ The incorrect spelling is usually shown in red type and the correct spelling is shown alongside it in black type.

▓ No meanings or other information about the words are given.

Here is an extract from *The Pergamon Dictionary of Perfect Spelling*

nest–nimbly			
nesesitey	necessity*	next/-of-kin	
neslin	nestling	nexus	
nest[1]/ling		ni	nigh
net[3]/ball		nibble[2]	
netha	neither	nibul	nibble[2]
nether		nice / ly / ness / r / st	
nettle[2]/rash		nicet *y* / ies	
netul	nettle[2]+	nich	niche
network		niche	
neumatick	pneumatic	nick[1]	
neural/gia		nickel	
neuritis		nickerbockers	knickerbockers
neurologist		nickers	knickers
neuron		nickle	nickel
neuro *sis* /tic		nicknack	knick-knack
neuter		nickname[2]	

— from *The Pergamon Dictionary of Perfect Spelling*, SRA Ltd

---

Why use a dictionary?

▓ It enables you to check any words in your writing that you are uncertain about.

▓ Used sensibly, it can increase your confidence when you are writing, as you know you have a reference source at hand.

How to use a dictionary

▓ Use your dictionary sensibly.

Don't: depend on it too much or you will find you start to check words that you aren't really uncertain about

use the dictionary to check the spelling of a word as you write.

18

techniques

Do: try to write the word

underline the word if you are unsure about it

check it later after you have proof-read your writing

proof-read all your writing

check any words you are uncertain about in a dictionary

always look for spelling mistakes in both your first and second draft.

■ When you check a word in a dictionary, make certain it is the word you want by checking its meaning as well as its spelling. This is particularly important for homophones. (See Chapter 5 *Memory Aids*, page 15.)

Dictionary skills

You'll find it quicker and easier to use a dictionary if you're aware of these points:

■ all entries in a dictionary are arranged in alphabetical order

■ at the top of each page there are two guide words

■ guide words show you the first and last words on that page

■ in most concise dictionaries, related words are shown within the entry.

Example: Within an entry for the word
deck
you might see listed
decked   decking   deckchair   deck-hand   clear the decks.

A brief meaning will be given for each associated word.

■ If you can't find a word in your dictionary, think of alternative beginnings for the word and try those.

Example: You are trying to check the spelling of a word beginning with a **k** sound.
Alternative beginnings could be
k as in **kidnap**
c as in **canoe**
ch as in **chaos**.

For you to do

Find a suitable dictionary. Either use one you already own that you find helpful or choose a new dictionary. Study your dictionary carefully. Think about:

■ the arrangement – look for guide words

■ an individual entry – how much information it gives about the word.

techniques

Combining the techniques

■ When you look up a long or difficult word, use your knowledge of dividing words into syllables. (See Chapter 3 *Taking Words Apart.*) This will allow you to concentrate on one part of the word at a time.

■ Say the word aloud and then write down the syllables.

Example: con / cen / trate

■ You can then try searching for the word by working through each syllable, letter by letter.

Creating your own dictionary

You have already been advised to list your target words. (See Chapter 1 *Introducing Spelling.*)

■ These target words can be entered into your own personal dictionary.

■ This can be a notebook that you divide into alphabetical sections.

■ You can enter your target words under the relevant letter.

■ Then you can easily find a word when you need to check its spelling or when you are deciding which words to learn.

Using a spell-check

■ If you use a word processor or computer, the spell-check can be a useful aid for spotting typing or spelling mistakes.

■ The spell-check will only be able to deal with words that have been entered into its dictionary so some correct spellings may be questioned, e.g. personal names, place names.

■ It won't be able to spot if you've made the wrong choice of word, e.g. 'practise' for 'practice'.

■ Many spell-checks are based on American spellings and may give an incorrect spelling or may try to correct a perfectly acceptable English spelling.

Checkpoints

- Using a dictionary is a valuable technique which will help you to present correctly spelt final drafts of your writing.
- Choose the right dictionary for you.
- Find out how your dictionary is arranged and what help it gives you with spelling.
- Always finish writing before you use a dictionary to check a spelling.
- Remember, the more you use a dictionary the easier and quicker it becomes to look up a word.

Chapter 7 **Knowing the Rules**

What are spelling rules?

- You may think that English spelling is illogical.
- However, approximately 85% of words follow a pattern or obey a rule.
- Spelling rules deal with groups of words that follow a particular pattern.

> **Example:** The letter **q** in a word is always followed by **u** and at least one other vowel.
>
> **qu**easy **qu**iver s**qu**abble e**qu**ip

- Often, as in the example above, you'll apply a rule to a word you're spelling without thinking about the rule.
- At other times, you may have to say the rule to yourself to check that you have used the correct spelling.
- Unfortunately, there are frequently exceptions to rules. You may have to use other techniques to remember these exceptions. (See Chapter 5 *Memory Aids*.)

Why are rules useful?

- One rule can be applied to hundreds, even thousands of words
- It's easier to learn a group of words that follow a rule than to learn each word separately.
- When you're proof-reading your writing and feel uncertain about the spelling of a word, you can check it against the appropriate rule.
- You may find that knowing rules gives you more confidence about spelling. Rules can help you understand the structure of the English language.

How to tackle rules

- It's not enough to learn a rule by heart. You need to understand how it works and be able to put it into practice.
- Be selective about the rules you learn. Learn those rules which:
  - will help you with your problem words
  - are simple to learn
  - apply to large numbers of words

▶ have few exceptions.

(See Chapters 8–12 for examples of such rules.)

▦ Try to learn and practise one rule at a time.

▦ When you read about a rule, try to express it in your own words. It's easier to recall then.

▦ When there is a list of exceptions to a rule, you need only learn those that are useful to you and that you'll use frequently.

| Some simple rules |

Rules for words ending in a *u* sound
an *i* sound
ful

▦ A **u** sound is an unusual ending for words in English.

▦ Word endings with a **u** sound are generally spelt either **ew** or **ue**.

> Examples: crew withdrew view threw
>
> subdue continue issue value

▦ And **i** sound at the end of words is usually made by **y** or **ie**.

> Examples: supply apply occupy
>
> die lie tie

▦ When **full** is added to the end of a word, an **l** in **full** is dropped.

> Examples: fretful cheerful wasteful
>
> faithful grateful

Checkpoints

▦ By learning rules and patterns in spelling, you will gradually begin to see what is possible and probable in English spelling.

▦ Learning a rule can be a quick way to learn the spelling of many words.

▦ Make sure you learn rules that are useful to you.

▦ Combine rules with other techniques and always use the approach that is best for you.

Chapter 8 **Plurals**

In this chapter you will be looking at rules for making singular words plural.
Singular means one of an item or one person, animal, etc.
Plural means more than one.

Examples:	**singular**	**plural**
	target	targets
	responsibility	responsibilities
	thief	thieves
	hero	heroes

What are the rules for plural spellings?

Add *s*

▦ Most words are made plural by adding **s**.

Examples:	option	friend	snake	castle
	option**s**	friend**s**	snake**s**	castle**s**

Add *es*

▦ Words which end in a 'hissing' sound (i.e. **ch, x, ss, z, zz, s, sh**) have **es** added to form the plural.

Examples:	*ch* ending	porch	porch**es**
	x ending	box	box**es**
	ss ending	guess	guess**es**
	z ending	waltz	waltz**es**
	zz ending	buzz	buzz**es**
	s ending	atlas	atlas**es**
	sh ending	flash	flash**es**

▦ You will notice that by adding **es** you are adding another syllable to the word so that you can hear the **es** ending.

Examples:	ad / dress *(two syllables)*	ad / dress / es *(three syllables)*
	bunch *(one syllable)*	bunch / es *(two syllables)*

Words ending in *y*

▓ If there is a vowel before the final **y** in a word, just add an **s** to form the plural.

Example: kidney *(e before final **y**)*   kidney**s**
               display *(a before final **y**)*   display**s**
               convoy *(o before final **y**)*   convoy**s**

▓ If there is a consonant before the final **y** in a word, change the **y** to **i** and add **es** when you make the word plural.

Examples: party   *(t before final **y**)*   part**ies**
             spy   *(p before final **y**)*   sp**ies**
             enquiry   *(r before final **y**)*   enquir**ies**
             bully   *(l before final **y**)*   bull**ies**
             galaxy   *(x before final **y**)*   galax**ies**
             enemy   *(m before final **y**)*   enem**ies**

Words ending in *ff*, *f* or *fe*

▓ With words that end in **ff**, add an **s** to make them plural.

Examples: cuff   cuff**s**   tariff   tariff**s**

▓ Words that end in **f** or **fe** are more difficult. Some form their plurals by adding **s**.

Examples: chief   chief**s**   gulf   gulf**s**
             roof   roof**s**   belief   belief**s**
             reef   reef**s**

▓ Other words ending in **f** or **fe** are made plural by changing the **f** to **v** and adding **es**.

Examples: shelf   shel**ves**   wolf   wol**ves**
             loaf   loa**ves**   leaf   lea**ves**
             thief   thie**ves**   wife   wi**ves**
             knife   kni**ves**   half   hal**ves**

▓ A few words ending in **f** can have either form in the plural.

Examples: dwarf   dwarf**s**   dwar**ves**
             scarf   scarf**s**   scar**ves**
             hoof   hoof**s**   hoo**ves**
             wharf   wharf**s**   whar**ves**

If you're uncertain about which plural form to use for an **f** or **fe** word, you can always check the spelling in a dictionary.

Words ending in *o*

▉ Some words which end in **o** add **s**, but others add **es** in the plural.

Examples: **add *s***

shampoo	shampoo**s**
trio	trio**s**
disco	disco**s**
studio	studio**s**

add *es*

volcano	volcano**es**
echo	echo**es**
tomato	tomato**es**
potato	potato**es**

▉ A few words which end in **o** can be spelt with either ending in the plural.

Examples: Eskimo   Eskimo**s**   Eskimo**es**
motto   motto**s**   motto**es**

▉ You will probably have to combine the rules with other techniques to remember the plurals of words ending in **o**.

❱ Try the visual technique – concentrate on the ending as you picture the word.

❱ Group words with **oes** endings together and make up a sentence:

He eats masses of potat**oes**, mang**oes** and tomat**oes**.

❱ Use your dictionary to check you've made the right choice.

Irregular plurals

Examples: man   m**en**   tooth   t**ee**th
child   child**ren**   louse   l**i**ce

▉ Such words are frequently used and well known so they don't usually present any problems.

Foreign words

▉ Some words taken from other languages still keep their original plural forms.

Examples:	**singular**	**plural**
	radius	rad**ii**
	criterion	criteri**a**
	larva	larv**ae**
	crisis	cris**es**

▉ Other words can have two plural forms: the original spelling and an anglicised one.

Examples:	**singular**	**original plural**	**anglicised plural**
	syllabus	syllab**i**	syllabus**es**
	fungus	fung**i**	fungus**es**
	formula	formul**ae**	formul**as**

There are no rules to help you with irregular plural words or foreign words. If you are uncertain about the plural form of any such words, then check the spelling in a dictionary.

Why are these rules useful?

- The rules for making words plural cover a large number of words: by learning the rules you will be able to spell a wide range and number of words.
- The rules for plurals have few exceptions.
- You can learn the exceptions to the rules by using other techniques.

Combining the techniques

- Throughout this chapter we have given you suggestions about other techniques you can combine with learning the rules.
- These include:
  - grouping words together
  - devising memorable phrases or sentences
  - using a dictionary.

Checkpoints

- The most common way to form a plural is to add **s**.
- Most other ways are covered by the rules given in this chapter.
- Remember, concentrate upon one rule at a time.
- Check that you have learnt a rule by saying it in your own words and testing it out on suitable words from your list of target words.
- Irregular plurals and foreign plurals need to be learnt using other approaches.
- You do not need to learn all the exceptions to rules, only those that are useful to you.

Chapter 9 **Suffixes**

In Chapter 8 you were shown how to make singular words plural, by adding **s** or **es**. You saw that sometimes the spelling of the root word changes when it is made plural.

This chapter looks at how adding other suffixes can affect the spelling of a root word.

What is a suffix?

> **suffix**   a syllable or other addition at the end of a word

— from *Chambers Twentieth Century Dictionary*

- A suffix may begin with a vowel (a vowel suffix) or a consonant (a consonant suffix).
- When a suffix is added to a word it doesn't necessarily change the meaning of the word.
- The suffix makes the root word 'fit' the way we wish to use it in the sentence.

Examples:	root word	suffix	new word
	book	-let	book**let**
	wake	-ing	wak**ing**
	immediate	-ly	immediate**ly**
	glory	-ous	glori**ous**
	employ	-ee	employ**ee**
	fit	-ed	fitt**ed**
	council	-or	council**or**

- The same suffix can be added to a variety of words.

Examples:	-**est**	bigg**est**
		bright**est**
		witti**est**

- More than one suffix can be added to a word.

Examples: joy**fulness**   effort**lessly**

                   /   \   /   \

           -ful   -ness   -less   -ly

28

Why is it useful to know about suffixes?

▓ The rules are clear and cover a large number of words with few exceptions.

▓ By recognising suffixes and knowing how they are added to words:

⟩ you can avoid many of the common spelling mistakes which are made when suffixes are added to root words, e.g forgetting to drop the final **e**:

advertise+-ing   advertis**ing**

⟩ you will find the technique for dividing long words up into syllables even more useful.

What are the rules for suffixes?

The rules
- no change
- the doubling rule
- the silent **e** rule
- the **y** to **i** rule
- the **l** rule
- the double syllable rule.

No change

▓ In most instances, the suffix is added directly to the root word with no change made to the spelling.

Examples: hard+-ship   hard**ship**
visit+-ing   visit**ing**

The doubling rule

▓ This rule applies to words that have

one syllable
one short vowel
one final consonant.

Examples: The vowel is short in these words:

can short **a**	beg short **e**	fit short **i**
hot short **o**	mug short **u**	

wet has   ***one*** syllable
one short vowel **e**
one final consonant **t**

rules and patterns

■ When you add a suffix beginning with a vowel to a root word that fits the 'one, one, one' pattern, you double the final consonant of the root word. Remember **y** can be a vowel too.

Examples: wet+-er   we**tt**er
          chat+-y   cha**tt**y
          stop+-ing   sto**pp**ing
          dim+-er   di**mm**er
          sun+-y   su**nn**y
          slip+-ed   sli**pp**ed

The silent *e* rule

■ Drop the final silent **e** from a root word when you add a vowel suffix.

Examples: rate+-ed   rat**ed**
          place+-ing   plac**ing**
          spice+-y   spic**y**
          invite+-ation invit**ation**

Exceptions

■ There are a few exceptions to the silent **e** rule and if you learn them, whole groups of words become easier to spell.

1 In words ending -**ce** or -**ge**, the **e** is kept when the suffixes -**able** or -**ous** are added, in order to keep **c** and **g** soft (sounding like **s** and **j**).

Examples: notice+-able   notic**e**able
          courage+-ous   courag**e**ous

You can find out more about hard and soft **c** and **g** in Chapter 12.

2 There are a very few root words which keep the **e** before a vowel suffix.

Examples: acr**e**age   dy**e**ing
          sing**e**ing   glu**e**y

3 A few words can be spelt with or without an **e**.

Examples: sizeable   sizable
          likeable   likable
          loveable   lovable
          ageing   aging
          queueing   queuing
          mileage   milage

■ You have been shown several exceptions to the rule, but on most occasions the silent **e** is dropped before a vowel suffix.

If you are unsure whether a word follows the rule, try writing the word both ways. Choose the spelling that looks right. Check the spelling in a dictionary if you are still uncertain.

The *y* to *i* rule

This follows the rule for making **y** words plural (see Chapter 8 *Plurals*).

If the root word has a consonant before the final **y**, change to **y** to **i** when you add a suffix. This rule applies whether you are adding a vowel suffix or a consonant suffix.

Don't change the **y** to **i** if you are adding -**ing**. You would have two **i**s together.

Examples: *carry* has a consonant before the **y**.
Add -er and it becomes **carrier**.
Add -ed and it becomes **carried**.
Add -ing and it becomes **carrying**.

heavy+-ness heaviness
apply+-ed applied
busy+-ly busily
pity+-ful pitiful

The *l* rule

This rule applies to two-syllable words which end in **l**.

If there is one vowel before the final **l**, double the **l** when you add a vowel suffix.

Examples: *Signal* has two syllables: sig / nal
There is one vowel before the final **l**.
Double the **l** *when you add* **ing**: signalling

label+-ing labelling
expel+-ed expelled
travel+-er traveller

There are a few exceptions to this rule.

Examples: brutal+-ity brutality
legal+-ise legalise
civil+-ise civilise

rules and patterns

The double syllable rule

When you add a vowel suffix to a root word that has

two syllables
one final consonant
one short vowel before the final consonant,

double the final consonant if the stress falls on the second syllable.

Examples: *Say the word **occur** aloud.*
You should hear that you stress the second syllable.
(Your voice becomes louder and stronger.)
*When you add **ing** to occur, the **r** is doubled:* occur**r**ing

forgot+-en   forgo**tt**en
equip+-ed   equi**pp**ed
begin+-ing   begi**nn**ing

The rules for double-syllable words are quite difficult. You need to be able to hear which syllable you stress in the word.

If you have problems, don't despair. Be aware of the rule and use your dictionary to check the spelling if you are uncertain.

Checkpoints

Remember: in most instances the spelling of the root word doesn't change when you add a suffix.

If the rules for suffixing are new to you, look back through this chapter and decide which rules are most useful to you.

Tackle one rule at a time.

If you find a rule difficult to remember, try other techniques for learning the spelling of those words.

Refer to the appropriate part of this chapter whenever you have difficulty with a particular rule for adding a suffix.

Chapter 10 **Prefixes**

What is a prefix?

▨ A prefix is a group of letters added to the beginning of a root word.

Examples: **un-** + true = untrue   **mis-** + use = misuse
                  ╱   ╲   ╱   ╲
               prefix   root word   *prefix   root word*

▨ A prefix changes the meaning of the root word it is added to.

Examples: **true**   *means 'genuine'*
          untrue *means 'false'*

Why is it useful to know about prefixes?

▨ Knowing about prefixes will help you with spelling:
  ▸ you will be more successful at dividing words into syllables if you can recognise prefixes
  ▸ by combining your knowledge of prefixes and suffixes (see Chapter 9 *Suffixes*), you will find it easier to build up and spell long words.
▨ Knowing the meaning of a prefix can also help you to work out the meaning of an unfamiliar word. (See Chapter 17 *Reading and Vocabulary*.)

What are the rules for prefixes?

No change
▨ Adding a prefix to most words is quite straightforward:
  ▸ the spelling of the word does not change
  ▸ the spelling of the prefix does not change.

Examples:

prefix	root word	new word
dis-	similar	**dis**similar
un-	necessary	**un**necessary
il-	legal	**il**legal
up-	stairs	**up**stairs
under-	ground	**under**ground
re-	union	**re**union
inter-	national	**inter**national
super-	natural	**super**natural

Common mistake

■ You will notice that, in words such as **dissimilar, unnecessary** and **illegal**, the last letter of the prefix is the same as the first letter of the root word. Sometimes you may forget to include both of these letters in the new word.

■ Remember, the spelling of neither the prefix nor the root word will change when they are put together as one word.

Examples: **dis-** satisfy = **dis**satisfy
solve = **dis**solve

ir- relevant = **ir**relevant
regular = **ir**regular

mis- spent = **mis**spent
spell = **mis**spell

im- mature = **im**mature
moral = **im**moral

Changes in spelling

■ The spelling of a few prefixes alter when they are added to certain root words.

Examples:

■ You will notice that:

▶ when the prefix **all** is added to a word, one **l** is always dropped

▶ when **well** is added to *some* words, one **l** is dropped

▶ but in words with a hyphen the prefix **well** remains unchanged.

Choosing the right prefix

▓ Some prefixes have a similar sound, for example **im-** and **in-**.

▓ If you are uncertain whether you have chosen the correct prefix:

▶ listen carefully to the sound of the new word and decide which prefix sounds right

▶ remember the prefix **in-** is never used before **p** or **m** – the prefix **im-** is always used before these letters

▶ check your choice in a dictionary. (You will need to know whether your dictionary shows words that can be made by adding prefixes under the root word, or whether they are all listed under the prefix.)

▓ Sometimes if you know the meaning of a prefix it can help you to make the correct choice.

Example: **ante-** *means 'before'*
           anti- *means 'against'*

If you want to write the word meaning 'before birth', you would choose the prefix **ante-** for **antenatal**.

For you to do

Use the correct prefix (**un-, in-, ir-, im-, il-,** or **dis-**) to form the opposite of each of these words:

dependent believe patient liberal audible rational
certain modest offensive manageable orderly perfect

Checkpoints

▓ The rules for adding prefixes are very simple.

▓ Knowing the rules and recognising prefixes can give you confidence to build up and write longer words.

▓ It will also help when you take long words apart to tackle their spelling. (See Chapter 3 *Taking Words Apart*.)

rules and patterns

- The order in which **i** and **e** occur in words often causes problems.
- You may know there is rule for this pattern but you may not know the complete rule.

What is the rule?

- **i** before **e** except after **c**, but only in words where these letters make a long **e** sound.
- A long **e** sound is the same as the letter **e** name or the sound of **ee** in 'teeth'.
- You need to listen to the sound that the **i** and **e** combination make, and then follow the rule.

Examples:

- In each of these words there is a long **e** sound, so **i** comes before **e**.

achieve — diesel

hygiene —— ie —— belief

shriek — niece

- In these words there is a **c** before the long **e** sound, so the pattern is spelt **ei**.

ceiling

receive — deceit

ei

receipt — conceit

conceive

- In these words there is no long **e** sound, so the pattern is **ei**.

their — foreign

eight — ei

leisure — height

weird

36

Exceptions
- There are very few exceptions to this rule.
- In each of these words the long **e** sound is spelt **ei**:

 counterf**ei**t
 prot**ei**n
 caff**ei**ne
 s**ei**ze

- The following sentence may help you to remember these exceptions.
 He seized the counterfeit protein and caffeine.
- You may or may not pronounce the following words with a long **e** sound. If you do, they can also be considered as exceptions to the rule. They are spelt **ei**.

 either
 n**ei**ther

For you to do

Say each of these words aloud to test whether they are spelt **ie** or **ei**. All the words follow the rule. Complete each word with the correct combination, **ie** or **ei**.

th __ __ f	w __ __ ght	perc __ __ ve
rel __ __ f	n __ __ ghbour	v __ __ n
f __ __ ld	br __ __ f	gr __ __ ve
bes __ __ ge	pr __ __ st	p __ __ ce

Why is this rule useful?

- Many students have problems with **ie** and **ei** spellings.
- The complete rule is simple to apply – you just need to listen for a long **e** sound.
- By knowing the complete rule, you will be aware that there are very few real exceptions to the rule. Therefore, you should feel more confident about tackling such words.

Other *ie* combinations

- There are other instances when **i** and **e** occur together and there is no long **e** sound, but they are quite easy to remember.

Two separate sounds

■ In these words you can hear the **i** and **e** making separate sounds when you divide each word into syllables.

Examples: audience   au / di / ence   society   so / ci / et / y
convenient   con / ve / ni / ent   experience   ex / per / i / ence

■ If you have difficulty remembering this **ie** combination, you could try adapting the way you say the syllables. (See Chapter 4 *Adapting the Pronunciation.*)

Example: audience   au / di/ ence
Stress **di** with a long **i** sound, like the short name 'Di' for 'Diana'.

y rule words

■ In Chapter 9, you saw that when most suffixes are added to a word ending in a consonant before a final **y**, the **y** changes to **i**.

■ If you recognise the pattern of the **y** rule, you shouldn't have any difficulty with the order of **i** and **e** in such words.

Examples: reply   replies   replied   defy   defies   defied

cie words

■ In **cie** words where the **ci** makes a **sh** sound, **i** comes before **e**.

Examples: efficient   ancient   conscience
sufficient   species   conscientious

■ You could try learning these words in small groups, but remember they all share a **cie** pattern. For instance, group together **efficient** and **sufficient** – they share the **fficient** ending.

■ You may prefer to learn the words you need by adapting their pronunciation. For example, you could learn **conscience** by saying **con** and **science** as two separate words.

Checkpoints

■ Most **ie** and **ei** spellings can be learnt by knowing the complete rule and following it.

■ You can use different techniques for remembering the exceptions and other **ie** combinations.

■ We have given you some suggestions for approaches that may be successful for you.

- The letters **c** and **g** can have different sounds in different words.
- The different sounds may cause problems for you when you are spelling unfamiliar words.

What are the different sounds of *c* and *g*?

- The letter **c** has a hard **c** sound (the same sound as **k** makes) in these words:

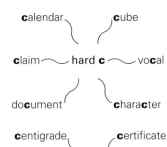

- The letter **c** has a soft **c** sound (the same sound as **s** makes) in these words:

- The letter **g** has a hard sound in these words:

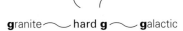

- The letter **g** has a soft sound (the same sound as **j** makes) in these words:

rules and patterns

What is the pattern?

▦ You need to look at the letter following the **c** or **g**:

▸ **c** and **g** usually make a soft sound when they are followed by **e, i** or **y**

▸ before the other vowels **a, o** and **u**, and before consonants, **c** and **g** will usually make a hard sound.

▦ The pattern for soft **g** at the beginning of words is not as reliable as the pattern for soft **c** at the beginning of words. There are a number of quite common words in which **g** followed by **e** or **i** has a hard sound.

Examples: **g**et   **g**ear   **g**eese   **g**eyser
            give   **g**ift   **g**iddy   **g**irl

Why is knowing this pattern useful?

▦ Knowing the pattern helps you to understand that:

▸ a **c** as well as an **s** can make **s** sound in a word

▸ a **g** as well as a **j** can make a **j** sound in a word.

▦ It gives you another option to try when you are attempting to spell a word with either an **s** or **j** sound in it.

▦ Knowing there are different ways of spelling an **s** and **j** sound is useful when you are checking a word in a dictionary.

▦ Understanding the pattern helps you to pronounce unfamiliar words.

Example: **c**ovalen**c**y
            The first **c** has a hard sound because it is followed by an **o**;
            the second **c** has a soft sound because it is followed by a **y**
            (**covalency** means the union of two atoms sharing a pair of electrons).

Other *c* and *g* patterns

Double *c* or *g*

▦ In some words where two **c**s occur together, the first letter of the pair makes a hard sound and the second a soft sound.

Examples: a**cc**ident   a**cc**ent   e**cc**entric   a**cc**ess
          su**cc**eed   va**cc**ination   a**cc**ept   a**cc**elerate

Keeping the *e*

▨ These words and a few others, are exceptions to the silent **e** rule you learnt in Chapter 9 *Suffixes*.

> servic**e**able notic**e**able peac**e**able
> manag**e**able courag**e**ous outrag**e**ous

▨ The **e** is usually dropped from silent **e** words when a vowel suffix is added, but if you dropped the **e** in the words above, you would pronounce them with a hard **c** or **g** sound. By retaining the **e**, you keep the soft sound.

xc words

▨ These words may cause you problems, as the **x** and the **c** tend to go together to make an **s** sound:

> ex**c**eed ex**c**ellent ex**c**ept ex**c**erpt ex**c**itement ex**c**ess

▨ If you have difficulties with these words, split them into syllables and use the visual technique to learn them. (See Chapter 2 *Looking at Words* and Chapter 3 *Taking Words Apart*.)

> ex / **c**eed ex / **c**ess ex / **c**ept

ce and *se* endings

▨ Both **ce** and **se** are possible letter patterns when an **s** sound is needed at the end of a word, but **ce** is more common than **se**:

> experien**ce**   nonsen**se**
> absen**ce**   increa**se**

▨ If you have difficulty with the endings of such words, try to learn them by grouping words with the same ending together in a sentence:

> A fal**se** promi**se** is nonsen**se**.

▨ There is a more about **ce** and **se** endings in the next chapter, Chapter 13 *Making the Right Choice*.

Checkpoints

▨ If you know the pattern for hard and soft **c**'s and **g**'s, you will find it easier to tackle many unfamiliar words.

▨ It will also help you when you're uncertain whether to use an **s** or a **c**, or a **g** or a **j** in a word.

▨ Remember the options and, if in doubt, check your choice of spelling in a dictionary.

rules and patterns

This chapter deals with words that you might confuse.

| What are the confusions? |

You may find words confusing because:

▨ they are homophones (words which *sound the same* but are *spelt differently* and have *different meanings*)

Example: beech   beach
              /   \
         a tree   seashore

▨ they have *a similar sound* but are *spelt differently* and have *different meanings*.

Examples: quite   quiet
               /   \
    completely *or* enough   still

           of   off
           /   \
    from *or* belonging to   away

| Why is it useful to know about these confusions? |

▨ It is easy to confuse homophones or similar sounding words when you're writing at speed in an exam.

▨ When you proof-read your writing, you might not spot your confusion because the word sounds the same as the one you meant to write.

▨ Many of these confusing pairs or groups of words are used frequently in writing so examiners will expect you to be aware of them and make the right choice.

▨ By knowing that they have different meanings and usage, you'll be aware of the need to check any you're uncertain about in a dictionary.

Common mistakes

There, their, they're

▨ **There** has two uses. It shows place, e.g.

> The car was parked over **there**.

and it is used with verbs, e.g.

> **There** are too many people in this lift.

▨ **Their** means 'belonging to them', e.g.

> This is **their** dog.

▨ **They're** is the shortened form of **they are** and is often used in informal writing, e.g.

> **They're** always on holiday at this time of year.

▨ If you aren't certain whether you've made the correct choice between these three words, ask yourself these questions.

> ▶ Would the words **they are** also make sense? If so, use the spelling **they're**.

> ▶ Does the word show ownership, i.e. is something being owned by 'them'? If so, the spelling **their** is correct.

> ▶ If neither of the above seems right in the sentence, you probably need **there**.

Its, it's

▨ **Its** means 'belonging to it', e.g.

> The cat lifted **its** injured paw.

▨ **It's** is short for **it is** or **it has**. The apostrophe shows that the letter **i** of **is** or the letters **ha** of **has** have been left out, e.g.

> **It's** a long time since I last saw you.

▨ When you are in doubt about either of these spellings, think of the meaning carefully: you can quite easily work out which to use.

Your, you're

This pair of words has the same pattern as **its** and **it's**.

▨ **Your** means 'belonging to you', e.g.

> **Your** writing is very clear.

▨ **You're** is the shortened form of **you are**, e.g.

> **You're** late.

▨ Remember: if the word you have written can be replaced by **you are**, then **you're** is needed.

rules and patterns

Two, to, too

Two is always used for the number 2, e.g.

> There were **two** people in the shop.

To has two uses: to show the direction 'towards', e.g.

> The passengers were all travelling **to** Edinburgh.

and with the verb to form the infinitive, e.g.

> They hope **to finish** by Wednesday.
>   /
>   *infinitive*

To is the most frequently used word in the group.

Too also has two meanings: **as well** or **also**, e.g.

> When I am in France, I shall visit Paris **too**.

or **excess** (**too** much), e.g.

> It was **too** hot for comfort.

▨ If you are uncertain whether you need **to** or **too**, check whether the word you want means 'an excess' or 'as well as' – if so, you need **too**.

Past, passed

This is the most difficult pair of homophones in the group.

▨ **Passed** has several meanings:

> *'went by'*   He **passed** the shop on his way to work.
>
> *'transferred'*   Nina **passed** the plate to him.
>
> *'got through'*   Taon **passed** his examinations last summer.
>
> *'agreed to'*   The council **passed** the plans after a vote.

▨ **Past** is also used in several different ways:

> *for time*   It is half-**past** eight
>
> *to mean 'beyond' or 'by'*   We walked **past** the stadium.
>
> *to mean 'bygone'*   He belongs to a **past** generation.

▨ If you are uncertain about whether you have made the right choice between **passed** and **past**, remember this rule.

  ▸ **passed** is a verb (a word of action)

  ▸ immediately in front of any verb you can place one of these words: **I, you, he, she, it, we**, or **they**

  ▸ test whether you need **passed** or **past** by putting one of the above words in front of it. If it makes sense, **passed** is the correct choice.

ce and *se* endings

- In Chapter 12 you saw that both **ce** and **se** are possible letter patterns when an **s** sound is needed at the end of a word.

- Some words are spelt with either a **ce** or **se** ending according to the way they are used in a sentence.

used as a noun	used as a verb
(a naming word)	*(an action word)*
practi**ce**	practi**se**
licen**ce**	licen**se**
prophe**cy**	prophe**sy**

- There is a rule to help you with these: the noun is spelt with a **c**, the verb with an **s**.

- To check your choice, ask yourself whether:

  - the word you have used is 'naming something' (a noun) and you can put **a** in front of it, e.g.

    Alan went to a cricket **practice** last night.

  - it is showing 'an action taking place' (a verb) and you can put **I, you, he, she, it, we** or **they** in front of it, e.g.

    They **practised** until they were exhausted.

For you to do

Each of the two words in these pairs has a similar sound and can be confused with the other. Make sure that you understand the differences in meaning by checking them in a dictionary.

affect	effect	addition	edition
eligible	illegible	aural	oral
loose	lose	imminent	eminent
personal	personnel	recent	resent

rules and patterns

Checkpoints

■ Be aware of words that have the same or a similar sound. You may like to list them in a personal dictionary. (See Chapter 6 *Using a Dictionary*.)

■ Tackle one pair or group at a time and learn the difference in spelling and meaning.

■ When you proof-read your writing, look out for incorrect choices.

■ If you're uncertain about your choice of word when you're writing, underline it and check it in a dictionary when you have finished that draft.

■ In this chapter we have made several suggestions about how you can remember which word to use. Chapter 5 *Memory Aids* also give you ideas to help you remember confusing pairs of words.

section 2
vocabulary

Chapter 14 **Introducing Vocabulary**

What is a 'good' vocabulary?

- It fits your needs.
- It gives you confidence.
- It helps you to understand.
- It is varied.
- It is exact.

Although it's difficult to be precise, there are approximately half a million words in the English language but, on average, most of us use less than 20,000 of these in our vocabulary.

Each of us has our own personal vocabulary, which we gain from our own special environment. Although we will probably continue to add new words to it throughout our lives, we have to make a special effort if we want our vocabulary to increase significantly.

Why is a 'good' vocabulary important?

- It helps you understand the exact meaning of what you hear and read.
- It allows you to speak and write easily and fluently.
- It makes your speech and writing more interesting, vivid, exact and effective.
- It enables you to use the correct tone to suit your audience and situation.
- You will gain higher marks for your coursework and in exams if you express yourself accurately.
- It enables you to complete writing tasks more quickly. If you have a wide variety of words to draw on, you will have the exact word for the situation.
- It can give pleasure to the people listening to you or reading your writing.
- It stops you confusing words or using them incorrectly.
- It can give you a range of precise words to use in formal writing tasks such as letters, reports, summaries and essays.
- It allows you to convey shades of meaning and colour, which are particularly useful in creative and descriptive writing.

How can you improve your vocabulary?

- Plan a campaign. It won't just happen.
- Be determined. Aim to research unfamiliar words you hear or read.
- Be alive to words.
- Be curious.
- Read widely and read texts that are demanding.
- Read actively and responsively. (See Chapter 17.)
- Use a dictionary. (See Chapter 15.)
- Make your own personal dictionary. (See page 50.)
- Use a thesaurus. (See Chapter 16.)
- Take part in word games.
- Listen actively.
- Understand prefixes. (There is a list on page 62.)
- Above all, practise.

To be successful, you need to be alive to words and curious about them. Try to find ways of encountering *new words* by listening; reading a wide range of good quality books, magazines and newspapers; and taking part in word games.

We use the term *new word* to refer to a word that isn't in your natural vocabulary. Your natural vocabulary consists of words that you use confidently because you understand their meaning and how to use them.

When you encounter a *new word*, you need to have a strategy for researching it.

Researching a new word

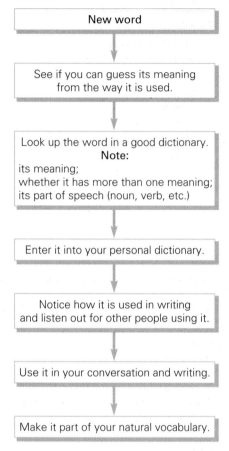

> **New word**
>
> See if you can guess its meaning from the way it is used.
>
> Look up the word in a good dictionary.
> **Note:**
> its meaning;
> whether it has more than one meaning;
> its part of speech (noun, verb, etc.)
>
> Enter it into your personal dictionary.
>
> Notice how it is used in writing and listen out for other people using it.
>
> Use it in your conversation and writing.
>
> Make it part of your natural vocabulary.

Making your own personal dictionary

Although this takes time, it is well worth doing. You will need an alphabetically indexed book or an alphabetically arranged filing system.

- Enter the word.
- Write down its meaning or meanings in your own words.
- Note the part of speech.
- Use a thesaurus to find alternative words with a similar meaning and note the main ones down.

Your entry may look something like this.

---

furore (noun)
        wild enthusiasm
        wild excitement
        an uproar
synonyms
        frenzy
        commotion
        disturbance
        outburst

For you to do

Read each of the sentences below.

■ Check that you really understand the meaning of each word underlined.

■ Could you clearly and accurately explain its meaning to someone who is unfamiliar with it?

■ Would you feel confident about using it in sentences of your own?

    1 The refugees were offered <u>succour</u> and support in neighbouring countries.

    2 There was such a <u>plethora</u> of political parties at the election that the peasants found it difficult to know who to vote for.

    3 Parents are <u>revered</u> in Chinese families.

    4 Holidays to faraway places are no longer a <u>prerogative</u> of the very rich.

    5 The plans are to <u>regenerate</u> derelict urban areas.

■ If you are uncertain of any of these words, follow the steps we gave you under the heading **Researching a new word** on page 50.

Checkpoints

■ You can improve your vocabulary if you work at it.

■ Learn five new words each day.

■ Read widely.

■ Listen carefully.

■ Develop an enquiring mind.

■ Use your dictionary and thesaurus sensibly.

■ Use new words whenever possible.

■ Start building up your personal dictionary *now*.

Chapter 15 Using a Dictionary

If you are determined to improve your vocabulary, you need at least one 'good' dictionary and you should feel confident about using it.

What is a 'good' dictionary?

- It covers a wide range of words.
- It gives all the meanings of a word.
- The definitions are detailed.
- It gives information about changes to spelling, pronunciation, parts of speech, origins of the word.

Why is a 'good' dictionary important?

Meaning It helps you to understand the meaning or meanings of a word.

Pronunciation It will show you how a word is pronounced.

Parts of speech It will tell you the part of speech of each entry. This helps you to use the word correctly.

Spelling It allows you to check the spelling of any word you are uncertain of.
It also gives you changes in spelling, for example when you add a suffix:

permit   permi**tt**ed   permi**tt**ing

Origin There is a brief history of each word so that you can appreciate the origin of each entry.

Related words and phrases When you look up a word, you will often find other words and phrases that are related to it. If you are curious and follow these up, it will also boost your vocabulary.

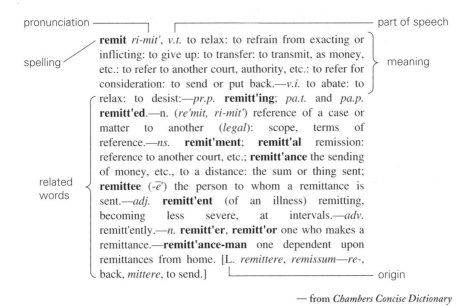

pronunciation ──────┐ ┌──────────────────────── part of speech

spelling

remit *ri-mit'*, *v.t.* to relax: to refrain from exacting or inflicting: to give up: to transfer: to transmit, as money, etc.: to refer to another court, authority, etc.: to refer for consideration: to send or put back.—*v.i.* to abate: to relax: to desist:—*pr.p.* **remitt'ing**; *pa.t.* and *pa.p.* **remitt'ed**.—*n.* (*re'mit, ri-mit'*) reference of a case or matter to another (*legal*): scope, terms of reference.—*ns.* **remit'ment**; **remitt'al** remission: reference to another court, etc.; **remitt'ance** the sending of money, etc., to a distance: the sum or thing sent; **remittee** (*-ē'*) the person to whom a remittance is sent.—*adj.* **remitt'ent** (of an illness) remitting, becoming less severe, at intervals.—*adv.* remitt'ently.—*n.* **remitt'er, remitt'or** one who makes a remittance.—**remitt'ance-man** one dependent upon remittances from home. [L. *remittere, remissum*—*re-*, back, *mittere*, to send.]

meaning

related words

origin

— from *Chambers Concise Dictionary*

Choosing the right dictionary for you

Consider:

- ▨ the size of the dictionary
- ▨ the layout of each entry
- ▨ the symbols used for pronunciation
- ▨ how clear and detailed the definitions are
- ▨ the size of print.

There is an excellent range of dictionaries available, so spend some time choosing one. You need one that fits your needs and is easy to use. Avoid the cheap 'special purchase' dictionaries which often have a limited range of words, incomplete and often misleading definitions, and give no information about changes to spelling when you add endings.

You may need more than one dictionary: a small one to carry around with you and a larger, more detailed one for reference at home.

Examples

These dictionaries are all very good:

The Concise Oxford Dictionary (Oxford University Press)
The New Penguin Dictionary (Penguin)
Chambers Concise Dictionary (Chambers)
Collins Concise Dictionary (Collins)
Collins Concise Dictionary Plus (Collins)
The Cassell Concise English Dictionary (Cassell)
Collins English Dictionary (Collins)
Oxford Reference Dictionary (Oxford University Press)

The last two dictionaries are larger and are designed as dictionaries/concise encyclopaedias. Many different fields of knowledge are included. There are also specialist dictionaries in many subjects which will give you help with technical or specialised vocabulary.

Understanding entries

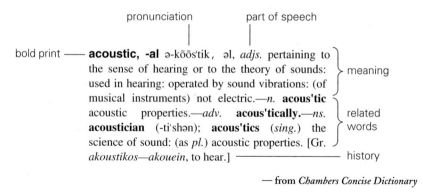

— from *Chambers Concise Dictionary*

If you are going to research words accurately and quickly, you need to be able to:

- find entries quickly, so make certain you know the order of the alphabet well and use the guide words at the top of each page in your dictionary
- understand the abbreviations and symbols that are used
- understand the roles of the various parts of speech so that you can appreciate how to use a particular word
- understand the definitions given.

What is the meaning?

The main part of any entry is taken up with the meaning of the word.

> pertaining to the sense of hearing or to the theory of sounds: used in hearing: operated by sound vibrations: (of musical instruments) not electric

— from *Chambers Concise Dictionary*

You will notice that each part of the explanation is separated from the next by a colon.

A definition can be difficult to understand for any of these reasons:

- It may contain other unfamiliar words within the explanation. If this is so, you will then have to look up these words too. (In the definition of **acoustic**, for instance, you may be uncertain about the exact meaning of **pertaining**.)
- Some words are difficult to explain in simple terms.
- The word may be about a subject of which you have little knowledge.

Advice

- Sometimes it is useful to look up the word in another dictionary, as you may find the definition there is more helpful.
- Don't try to remember the exact dictionary definition of a word. 'Translate' the definition into your own words. This will help you to understand, remember and feel comfortable with the word.
- Sometimes when you look up a word it has more than one meaning. It's important to consider all the options and not just choose the first part of the explanation.

Your research

It is useful to develop a procedure for new words. You were introduced to this idea in Chapter 14, page 50.

Before you look up the word in a dictionary:

- See if you can guess the meaning of the word from the context it is used in.
- Ask yourself whether it looks like another word you know. For example, the word **revere** may remind you of **reverend** or **reverence** and so help you to work out the meaning.
- Consider which part of speech it is. Use the sentence for clues.

When you use your dictionary:

- Look carefully at all the meanings or shades of meaning in the entry.
- Select the meaning that is appropriate for the situation. Does this definition make sense in your sentence?
- Check the part of speech.
- Check you are pronouncing the word correctly.
- Learn how to spell the word. Are their alternative ways of spelling the word? Are there any changes in spelling when you add endings?
- Check whether there are any related words that may be useful to you.
- Enter the word in your personal dictionary.

Checkpoints

- Choose a dictionary carefully.
- Learn how to use it effectively.
- Use it in a disciplined way.
- Always check unfamiliar words in a dictionary.
- Enter your findings in your personal dictionary.
- Use new words as much as possible in your conversation and writing and the words will become part of your natural vocabulary.

Chapter 16 Using a Thesaurus

▓ If you refer to a dictionary to find the meaning of 'thesaurus', you will find that it defines it as being 'a treasury or storehouse of knowledge'.

▓ Generally, when we refer to a thesaurus, we mean a book containing a collection of synonyms and antonyms.

Synonyms

▓ Synonyms are words that have a *similar* meaning to each other.

Examples: **mend** fix, restore, heal, rectify, improve, cure
effigy carving, image, statue, figure, icon, idol

▓ Remember, synonyms have *similar* meanings, not necessarily the same meaning.

▓ Consider carefully how a word is being used in a sentence before you replace it with a synonym.

Example: The camera took excellent photographs after it had been **mended**. ✓
The camera took excellent photographs after it has been **cured**. ✗

Antonyms

▓ Antonyms are words that have the opposite meaning to each other.

Examples: **nervous** confident, calm, equable, bold
spacious cramped, confined, narrow, small

▓ As with synonyms, a list of antonyms will reflect shades of meaning. You will need to select the one that is most appropriate for the sentence you are using it in.

Why is a thesaurus important?

▓ It helps you to develop your vocabulary.

▓ It can improve your writing and speaking skills.

▓ It enables you to express shades of meaning.

▓ It allows you to find a more precise word.

▓ It gives you a variety of words to chose from and helps you to avoid repeating the same word or words.

Types of thesauruses

Alphabetical arrangement

▓ These are easy to use – just like dictionaries. The words are arranged in alphabetical order.

▓ Beside each entry is a list of alternative words you could use. You can then choose the one or ones suitable for your situation.

▓ In some thesauruses there is also a list of antonyms at the end of some entries. In other thesauruses there is a separate section for antonyms.

Here is an entry from *Chambers Thesaurus.*

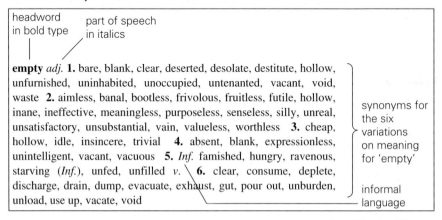

headword in bold type

part of speech in italics

empty *adj.* **1.** bare, blank, clear, deserted, desolate, destitute, hollow, unfurnished, uninhabited, unoccupied, untenanted, vacant, void, waste **2.** aimless, banal, bootless, frivolous, fruitless, futile, hollow, inane, ineffective, meaningless, purposeless, senseless, silly, unreal, unsatisfactory, unsubstantial, vain, valueless, worthless **3.** cheap, hollow, idle, insincere, trivial **4.** absent, blank, expressionless, unintelligent, vacant, vacuous **5.** *Inf.* famished, hungry, ravenous, starving *(Inf.)*, unfed, unfilled *v.* **6.** clear, consume, deplete, discharge, drain, dump, evacuate, exhaust, gut, pour out, unburden, unload, use up, vacate, void

synonyms for the six variations on meaning for 'empty'

informal language

— from *Chambers Thesaurus*

Roget's thesaurus

▓ We wouldn't recommend that you buy this type of thesaurus, as it is much more difficult to use.

▓ There may be occasions when you want to use one, as this type gives you a wider range of words and phrases. We suggest you look at a copy in your library.

Dictionaries of synonyms and antonyms

▓ Don't confuse these with general English dictionaries. They are just like alphabetical thesauruses as they give lists of synonyms and antonyms, although some may have a smaller variety of alternatives.

Examples: These are all easy to use and very good:
The *Collins Paperback Thesaurus in A–Z Form* (Collins)
Chambers Dictionary of Synonyms and Antonyms (Chambers)
Collins Pocket Thesaurus in A–Z Form (Collins)
Chambers Thesaurus (Chambers)
The Oxford Study Thesaurus (Oxford University Press)

Dictionaries versus thesauruses

- If you really want to improve your vocabulary, you need both a dictionary and thesaurus. They do different jobs.
- A dictionary gives you the meaning of a word. In a definition there will sometimes be synonyms but a thesaurus will give you a much wider range of synonyms.
- When you are using a thesaurus, you will often have to refer to a dictionary to check the meaning of an unfamiliar word. You should do this, as without this research your vocabulary can't grow.
- By using a dictionary and thesaurus together, you will avoid making mistakes, and find you can research words more effectively. It can be an exciting voyage of discovery!

Advice

- When you are planning a formal speaking task, or writing a letter, report or essay, it's best to use your thesaurus after you have written the first draft. Get your ideas down on paper first and, as part of your redrafting, underline any words that you aren't satisfied with. You may feel they are imprecise, dull, inappropriate or repetitive.
- Remember, only some of the synonyms or antonyms for an entry will be suitable for your situation.
- Check the meanings of any unfamiliar words in a dictionary.
- When you choose a word, consider your audience and the situation.
- Some of the synonyms or antonyms listed will have a colloquial use or be slang, so be careful in formal situations (see Chapter 19 *Conversational Words*).
- You may need to rephrase a sentence when you select a synonym to replace it.

Example: He spoke **well**.
          He was **articulate**.

Checkpoints

- An alphabetically arranged thesaurus is easier to use.
- You need a good dictionary and thesaurus if you are really serious about improving your vocabulary.
- Be careful to select the exact word for the situation.
- If you find words in your thesaurus that you are uncertain about, check them in your dictionary.
- Just as it is a good idea to keep a personal dictionary, it is useful to develop a personal thesaurus, and then the words that are useful to *you* are at your fingertips.

Chapter 17 **Reading and Vocabulary**

There is a clear relationship between reading and vocabulary. As Chapter 14 suggests, there are a number of ways to improve your vocabulary, but reading is probably the most effective method and for many people it is the most enjoyable. Chapter 14 encourages you to read actively and responsively.

What is active and responsive reading?

It is:

- reading a wide variety of texts
- reading sufficiently demanding material
- marking or noting down unfamiliar words as you read
- researching these words
- entering them into your personal dictionary
- using them as a natural part of your speaking and writing.

Why is reading important?

- It helps you to develop your vocabulary.
- You encounter and have to deal with unfamiliar words.
- Different authors use different vocabulary and structures to express themselves, which opens up a range of possibilities for you.

During your English coursework and in the exams, you have to read a range of texts and understand, question and respond to them. In other subjects you are also required to read and understand. A wide vocabulary can increase your understanding and enjoyment of what you read.

This can be called a reading circle.

Reading for pleasure

When we read for pleasure we want to enjoy the text and understand the subject matter, but gaining information isn't always our prime aim. This type of reading can be a valuable source of new words if the text is sufficiently demanding. Don't fail to take the opportunity to increase your vocabulary. Note down the words that are new to you or you don't fully understand. It may spoil your pleasure in reading if you keep stopping to look up words, so underline them or note them down as you go, and research them later.

Reading for information or study purposes

In this type of reading vocabulary is very important as:

▓ you will have to understand the text fully

▓ in order to read effectively and be able to recall the relevant points, you will need to have a complete understanding of the words

▓ you will probably encounter demanding passages containing unfamiliar or technical words.

It is essential you understand the information you read, so you will need to adopt a responsive approach to reading. By researching the new words you come across, you will extend your vocabulary.

How to tackle unfamiliar words

▓ Use the context – try to guess its meaning from the sentence in which it appears.

▓ Do you understand the meaning of the *prefix* or *root word*?

▓ Try to think of any related words.

▓ Refer to a dictionary.

▓ Record the word in your personal dictionary.

Root words

▓ A root word is a base word before a beginning (prefix) or ending (suffix) is added to it.

Prefixes

▓ A prefix is a group of letters added to the beginning of a word. A prefix alters the meaning of the root word.

▓ Understanding the meaning of individual prefixes is especially useful when you tackle unfamiliar words, as prefixes can provide vital clues to meaning.

Examples:

prefix	meaning	prefix	meaning
trans-	across	pre-	before
mono-	single	semi-	half
hyper-	over	mis-	badly
syn-	together	ante-	before
mal-	bad, badly	anti-	against
circum-	around	contra-	against
bi-	two	tri-	three

Related words

Once you are aware of root words and prefixes, you will notice how words belong to word families and share similar meanings.

Examples: **grate**ful   thankful
gratify   to please or indulge
gratuity   a gift in return for service
gratuitous   performed without charge, freely given

All the words above belong to a word family based on the idea of giving pleasure or wishing to express pleasure. They are all based on the Latin word **gratus** meaning pleasing or thankful.

▨ By understanding the meaning of one or two words in a family, you can often make a reasonable attempt at working out the other words.

Checkpoints

▨ Become a more active reader. Read widely and read texts that are demanding.

▨ Adopt a more critical and questioning style of reading. For instance, ask yourself these questions:

What does this word mean?

Why has the author used this word?

What other words could he or she have chosen?

▨ Never miss an opportunity to research an unfamiliar word. Reading is a prime source for enlarging your vocabulary.

Chapter 18 Being Accurate

What does 'being accurate' mean?

- Accuracy involves using the correct information, spelling, punctuation, grammar and vocabulary. In this chapter we will be concentrating on correct vocabulary.
- Being accurate in speech and writing involves expressing yourself clearly and without making mistakes.
- This chapter looks at some areas of vocabulary which can cause difficulties, such as:

    common confusions
    'precise' words
    colloquial language
    clichés
    tautology
    verbosity

Why is accuracy important?

- It allows others to understand exactly what you say or write.
- It gains you higher marks in all subjects, both in coursework and exams.
- It's polite – it shows consideration for your audience.
- It helps you to be effective. There are situations where making mistakes lets you down.

Common confusions

Which is correct?

    The drunken driver **flaunted** the law.
    The drunken driver **flouted** the law.

It's easy to confuse the two words because they look visually similar and sound similar.

    flaunt display ostentatiously or offensively; wave proudly
    flout show scorn of; treat with contempt

By comparing the dictionary definitions above, you will see that **flouted** is correct.

63

For you to do

Here are some more pairs of words than can be confused. Check any you are uncertain about in a dictionary and then note them down in your personal dictionary.

To increase your vocabulary further, you could also check them in a thesaurus and enter them in your personal thesaurus.

judicious	judicial	alternate	alternative
disinterested	uninterested	official	officious
momentary	momentous	abuse	misuse
adverse	averse	comprehend	apprehend
credible	creditable	oral	aural
illegible	ineligible	illusion	allusion

If there are pairs of words that you know you often feel confused by, then make a list of them with their correct definitions so that you can use them as a check when you redraft any piece of work.

'Precise' words

Look at these two sentences. Why are they incorrect?

1 The vote was almost unanimous.

2 Their house is very unique.

Sentence 1 Unanimous means 'all of one opinion; with no disagreement.' A vote is unanimous if everyone agrees, so a vote is either 'unanimous' or 'not unanimous'.

Sentence 2 Unique means 'the only one of its kind' so the house cannot be *very* unique. The word 'very' is unnecessary.

Here are some other words that are exact in themselves: they are absolute. They don't need other words to qualify them.

necessary   immaculate   essential   silent

You shouldn't use words like those below to qualify them.

very   merely   totally   almost   extremely   more   less

In informal situations such mistakes are acceptable. We all use them to create effect and gain our listeners' attention. However, in formal writing or speaking you should avoid such mistakes.

Colloquial language

> **colloquial** [kolOkwi-al] adj used in informal speech, characteristic of everyday conversation ~ **colloquially** adv ~ **colloquialism** n colloquial word or expression.

— from *Penguin English Dictionary*

Examples: He's always **stirring up trouble**.
My tutor **comes up with** some really **half-baked** ideas sometimes.
It seems a **bit dodgy** to me.
Exams **get up my nose**.
She has a **dicky** heart.

■ Colloquial language is fine for informal situations, but you should avoid it in formal situations.

■ Using colloquial words and phrases stops you using more interesting and exact words and doesn't allow you to develop your vocabulary.

■ Most dictionaries identify words and phrases which are colloquial, so use a dictionary if you are uncertain about words.

Clichés

cliché (kleeshay) n. stereotyped, hackneyed expressions

See if you can spot the clichés in this newspaper report.

Council Announces Spending Breakthrough

Yesterday Councillor E. Loveday announced cuts in spending amounting to a staggering £200,000. 'These saving have been made,' Councillor Loveday declared, 'by swingeing cuts in costs. No stone has been left unturned. Every avenue has been explored. In this day and age, our residents have a right to expect the Council to come up with a blueprint for success to ensure high standards of service at a rock bottom price.'

■ We so frequency hear of 'breakthroughs', 'swingeing' cuts, 'blueprints' for success, etc., that the words lose their impact.

■ Avoid clichés and use simple, expressive words or phrases.

Tautology

> **tautology** [tawtoloji] *n* unnecessary repetition of the same idea in different words.

— from *Penguin English Dictionary*

Examples: connect **up**, repeated it **again**, combined **together**, descended **down**, **new** innovation, you **first** begin, collaborated **together**

The words in bold print are tautologous: they are unnecessary as they repeat an idea. For example, **collaborate** means 'work together', so you don't need the word **together**.

■ Every word in a sentence should fulfil a useful function. Check your writing so that you can remove any unnecessary words that repeat an idea.

Verbosity

This is when you use a large number of words or long, complicated words or phrases to express a simple idea.

Examples: He replied in the affirmative.
In view of his lack of punctuality, his employment was terminated.

It would be more simple and effective to write:
He said, 'Yes!'
As he was unpunctual, he was dismissed.

Checkpoints

■ Be aware of the types of mistakes all of us can make.

■ Remember that there are words and phrases that are more suited to informal than formal situations.

■ Consider your audience and purpose. Do you need a precise vocabulary to create a formal tone for a formal situation?

Chapter 19 Conversational Words

What are conversational or colloquial words?

■ These are words that are more suited to informal situations and should be avoided in formal writing or speaking.

Teachers and examiners of GCSE English often criticise candidates for using colloquial words in formal writing situations.

Why is it important to avoid them?

Choosing the appropriate vocabulary is like dressing correctly for an occasion. When you go anywhere, you choose your clothes carefully to suit the occasion and the people you will be with. You don't want to be overdressed for an informal event or underdressed for a formal occasion.

■ A formal situation and audience demands a formal vocabulary. You should avoid conversational words.

■ This chapter:

　◗ makes you aware of avoiding colloquial words for formal situations

　◗ gives you examples of some colloquial words to avoid

　◗ outlines alternative, more exact words you could use instead.

Mad

> I went mad when my sister borrowed by walkman.
> Tidying my room makes me mad.
> I'm mad with Darren.

■ In these examples **mad** is being used in a colloquial way meaning 'angry'.

■ The true meaning of **mad** is 'insane' or 'recklessly foolish'.

Why use **mad** when there are so many other words that mean angry?

irate	incensed	displeased
enraged	irritated	peevish
outraged	infuriated	riled
affronted	indignant	annoyed
vexed	furious	disturbed
exasperated	fuming	offended

▓ By choosing your words carefully, you can find the exact word to express the right degree of anger. Do you want to be 'irritated' or 'annoyed', or 'fuming' or 'furious'?

For you to do

If any of the words in the list on the previous page are new to you, look them up in a dictionary and make a note of them. For example

▓ **Cross,** when used to show displeasure, is another chatty word to avoid.

> I am always cross on Monday mornings.

Tell off / told off

> Abdul was told off by Miss Hedges.
> I will tell you off if you do that again.
> He was given a good telling off when he got home.

▓ **Tell off** means 'scold' or 'chide'.

What other words could you use?

reprimand	nag	censure
chastise	reproach	discipline
reprehend	revile	lecture
castigate	admonish	remonstrate with
correct	rebuke	reprove
upbraid	berate	vituperate

All of these words have a slightly different meaning so select the best word for the situation.

Fed up or boring

▓ When you are displeased with someone or something, you may say you are **fed up**. Although it gives a general picture of how you feel, it isn't very exact.

Alternatives: I'm fed up with work.
> I find work **tiring** and **tedious**.

> Emma was fed up with his interference and his unwelcome offers of help.

Emma was **annoyed by** his interference and his unwelcome offers of help.

The nurse was fed up with climbing the steep flight of steps to the pharmacy.

The nurse was **exhausted by** climbing the steep flight of steps to the pharmacy.

Why are you bored?
Is someone or something:

wearisome	monotonous	stale
commonplace	routine	unvaried
mundane*	tiresome	irksome*
tedious*	repetitious*	humdrum?
unexciting	uninteresting	

For you to do

Use each word marked with an asterisk in an interesting sentence.

Funny

▨ The real meaning of **funny** is 'amusing'.
▨ We also use it in a colloquial way to mean 'odd'.

Do you know how **funny** is being used in each of these sentences?

'Men Behaving Badly' is a very funny programme.
Matthew's very funny.
That's funny!

It's impossible to be certain. Each sentence is rather vague.

▨ Never use **funny** in its colloquial sense in formal situations.
▨ You can also use a variety of words instead of **funny** when you want to describe something or someone as 'amusing'.

Alternatives to **funny** when it means 'amusing':

absurd	droll	facetious
ludicrous	humorous	jocular
hilarious	comical	ridiculous
mirth-provoking	entertaining	

For you to do

Use a thesaurus to add to the list of words in the frame below. If you are uncertain about any of the words you find, check them in a dictionary.

Words to use instead of **funny** when you want to describe someone, something or somewhere as 'odd' or 'strange':

unusual	outlandish	awkward
eccentric	exceptional	unfamiliar
unconventional	bizarre	
alien	remarkable	

Don't use **odd** or **strange** instead of **funny** when you want to describe something as 'unusual' or 'remarkable'. They are as imprecise as **funny**. Your audience will have a clearer picture if you choose more descriptive words.

A lot of / lots of

There is often a lot of trouble at the 'Dog and Pheasant' on Saturday nights.
Lots of people worked on the land during the eighteenth century.
Gavin earns lots of money.

It is quite acceptable to use these words in informal situations; formal situations need more precise vocabulary.

At times, you will be able to quote an exact number and it's best to do so wherever possible. Where you can't state the exact number and just want to indicate a large number, you can choose from a variety of words like the ones below:

abounding	endless	infinite
countless	unnumbered	profuse
numerous	myriad	overflowing
numberless	abundant/abundance	multitudinous
innumerable	copious	teeming

For you to do

Go back through this chapter and use a dictionary to check the meaning of any words you have forgotten or are unfamiliar with. Try to use them in your writing and speech so that you remember them.

Checkpoints

- Choose exact vocabulary for formal situations and audiences.
- Use a variety of words.

Chapter 20 **Overused Words**

This chapter:

■ encourages you to replace overused words with a more varied vocabulary

■ introduces you to some alternative words you could use.

What are overused words?

■ These are words that we use so often in speech and writing that their meaning can become blunted.

Why is it important to use a range of words?

■ It makes your speech and writing more vivid and precise.

Nice

> It's a nice town.
> Danny had a nice holiday.
> My sister is nice.

■ You will hear comments like this every day. They are part of our natural conversation, but do they give us much information?

■ Think about why something or someone is **nice**:

> It's an **attractive** town.
> Danny had a **relaxing** holiday.
> My sister is **understanding**.

By replacing the word **nice** in each of these sentences, you now have a clearer picture.

■ In writing, you may try to be even more exact and descriptive by using additional words to replace **nice**.

> It is a **quiet** and **attractive** town.

Lovely and **beautiful** are used frequently too when we want to describe someone or something as 'very pleasing' or 'delightful'.

There is a range of synonyms you can use according to the degree of 'delight' you want to express:

pleasing	enjoyable	delightful
agreeable	attractive	fine
appealing	admirable	
pleasant	pretty	

In other situations you may wish to use words that show why someone or something is 'nice', 'lovely' or 'beautiful', e.g.

> My boss is nice.

Do you like him because he is:

> well-mannered? considerate? amiable?
> generous? friendly? amusing?

Nasty

This can mean the opposite of 'nice', 'lovely' or 'beautiful'.

You could use these alternatives:

unpleasant	despicable	loathsome
disgusting	malodorous	obnoxious
repellent	odious	spiteful
vile	repugnant	vicious
noisome	obscene	

Although all these words can be used to replace **nasty**, different words will fit different situations.

Good and bad

- **Good** is used to describe someone or something as having desirable or suitable qualities, and **bad** is an antonym for **good**. Both of these words are used very frequently. Try to think of more exact words to replace them.

- Many of the words that can be used to replace **nice** could also be used to replace **good**. Those given for **nasty** could be alternatives for **bad**.

Big or large and little or small

Size is difficult to describe as each of us has a different perception of:

> a big problem   a large meal
> a little further   a small room

- If you want to describe size exactly, you have to use precise measurements or a comparison.

> He farms a 9,500 acre estate.
> I only want a little piece – half the size of Tasmin's slice.

■ We also use this group of words to describe someone's age.

big *meaning* 'grown-up', 'mature', 'adult'

small or **little** *meaning* 'young'

If you don't want to give precise measurements or ages, there is a range of words you could use for **big** or **large**, according to the situation:

abundant	valuable	considerable
powerful	huge	influential
burly	mammoth	voluminous
extensive	massive	prominent
significant	spacious	roomy
substantial	sizable	prodigious
ample	colossal	bulky
plentiful	immense	important

For you to do

Look up **little, small** and **tiny** in a thesaurus. Make a list of the alternative words you could use. Use a dictionary to check any words that you are unfamiliar with.

Interesting

Mull is an interesting island to visit.
'An Inspector Calls' is an interesting play.
Tahir is an interesting person.

Interesting *means* 'engaging the attention' *or* 'exciting emotion or passion'

We each have different ideas about why someone or something is **interesting**. Can we use other words to be more exact?

Is it interesting because it is:

captivating	exciting	engaging
inspiring	amusing	absorbing
diverting	gripping	stimulating
entertaining	intriguing	enigmatic
provocative	fascinating	unusual
engrossing	spell-binding	compelling?
riveting	appealing	

Got and *get*

I get up at 7am.
Sharma gets her clothes at 'Ragtime'.
Rory got bitten by a dog.

▨ These words can become monotonous as we all use them so frequently in our speech and informal writing.

Get and **got** are used in many different ways:

get a reputation for	*acquire*	get old	*become*
get a coat	*fetch* or *buy*	got a present	*received*
got a meal	*prepared*	got the meaning of	*understood*

▨ There are many words that you can choose to replace **get** and **got** according to the context in which they are used.

For you to do

▨ Use your dictionary to check the meaning of any words in this chapter that are new to you. Write a simple definition of each word in your personal dictionary. If possible, use each word in a sentence so that you become accustomed to using each new word.

▨ There may be other words in this chapter that you have encountered before but do not feel totally confident about using. Check these in your dictionary too.

Checkpoints

▨ Be aware of words that are overused. There are many more than appear in this chapter.

▨ Make a conscious effort to choose alternative words to replace overused words.

Chapter 21 | Being Descriptive

What does being descriptive involve?

It involves:

- selecting the most apt and descriptive vocabulary to express your ideas and observations
- using suitable words to create atmosphere and clarity.

Why is it important to be descriptive?

- There are many occasions when you want to use words effectively to create a colourful image in for example, speech, essays, personal writing and informal letters.
- You want to describe your feelings and experiences accurately and give interest and enjoyment to your audience.
- A careful choice of descriptive words can also make your formal writing more forceful and persuasive.
- This chapter:
  - looks at several themes and shows you how to choose words that will help you to build atmosphere and clarity of description
  - gives you the opportunity to practise writing short passages based on the vocabulary and example passages we give you.

Quietness

- Which of these two sentences is more effective?

  He walked quietly through the quiet building.
  He walked noiselessly through the silent, peaceful building.

- In the second sentence, we begin to feel the stillness and tranquillity of the scene – **quietly** and **quiet** fail to convey the depth of the silence.

Words you could use to create an idea of 'quietness':

hushed	subdued	meek
shy	tranquil	gentle
soundless	calm	serene
unpretentious	contented	docile
retiring	motionless	smooth
secret	unobtrusive	conservative
imperturbable	sedate	isolated
undisturbed	plain	restrained
mild	simple	untroubled

For you to do

Use words from the frame above and select other words from your thesaurus to continue the passage below. You may like to describe the room itself or the scene through the window.

> I was aware that I had lowered my voice to an almost inaudible whisper as I spoke to her. She seemed to be surrounded by an aura of stillness which I was reluctant to disturb. Her shy smile, calm manner and gentle voice unsettled me.

Darkness

In the passage below the writer is trying to create the atmosphere of a dilapidated city at night.

> Henry strode hurriedly along the shadowy street, curbing an increasing desire to look over his shoulder. Around him dim, dingy houses crowded together, their windows broken and paint peeling. He shivered. Between the houses, in dark alleyways, menacing shadows took shape. Peering anxiously ahead, he was relieved to see a distant light whose welcoming glow penetrated the surrounding gloom.

Other words which you could use to describe a scene like this:

murky	unlit	sombre
shady	dusky	overcast
dismal	obscure	deserted
drab	abandoned	destroyed
glowering	neglected	threatening
derelict	sunless	mournful
forsaken	gloomy	

For you to do

See if you can create a similar atmosphere by writing a short passage about a young child lost in fog on a chill November evening. Some of the words in the frame on the previous page will help you to describe the denseness of the fog. Some words to describe the chill of the evening:

bleak	wintry	freezing
biting	frosty	icy
raw	bitter	

Words to help you convey the child's fear:

bewildered	helpless	terrified
forlorn	solitary	panic-stricken
petrified	alarmed	

Contrasts

Sometimes we want to create contrasts. Here we are creating a contrasting picture of the same scene.

■ Compare these two lists of words, which conjure up very different impressions of a seascape:

calm	smooth	stormy	tumultuous
tranquil	idyllic	tempestuous	foam
peaceful	undisturbed	turbulent	lash
placid	ripple	wild	surge
still	lap	harsh	crash

In this passage the scene changes from one of pace and tranquillity to that of storm and turmoil.

> In the pale, early morning light the tranquil sea beckoned; small boats rocked rhythmically in the breeze. The young girl plunged eagerly into the smooth water.
>
> As she drew level with the headland, the sun disappeared behind the threatening storm clouds. Waves, which had previously lapped over her, began to surge angrily against her. Squally showers swept across the water, and stinging rain blurred her vision.

For you to do

Describe a boat trip, contrasting the boat's quiet, steady exit from the harbour with the sudden rough conditions of the open sea.

These words may help you with the movement of the boat and sea:

glide   drift   flow   buffet   billow   swell
choppy   whirl   eddy   lurch   plunge   rock   pitch

Think also about the wind's strength:

breeze   breath of air   motionless   gust   bluster   rage   blast

Secretive movements

▨ In essays you are sometimes asked to write about a situation from a particular point of view. You should try to focus your description accordingly.

The following passage describes a cat trying to catch a bird. We follow the story first through the cat's and then the bird's actions.

> The emaciated cat stealthily stalked its unsuspecting victim. As the bird, sensing danger, nervously fluttered into a nearby holly bush, the cat skulked under an adjoining shrub, casting surreptitious glances at its prey.

> The bird, perching tensely on a twig and ready for flight at any moment, issued a series of high-pitched warning cries. The cat pounced. The bird, in a frenzy of beating wings, tried to rise. For a moment it seemed as if the cat had succeeded: a flurry of feathers drifted down but the bird rose higher and now, safe from the cat's grasp, seemed to hover for a while before triumphantly circling and flying swiftly away.

For you to do

Write a short description of an intruder creeping into a bedroom where the occupant is asleep.

▨ Describe the actions of the intruder, the awakening of the occupant and how the intruder makes his/her escape.

▨ Use suitable words from the passage above and ones from the frame below to help you. The words we used on page 77 of this chapter to describe 'quietness' may also be useful.

▨ You may decide to create a contrast between the intruder's slow, noiseless entry to the room and his hurried, noisy escape.

conceal	unseen	tremble
sneak	disguise	slither
slinking	prowl	silent
squirm	fluster	slid
creep	unsuspecting	
sly	muffle	

Fighting

In this description of a playground fight, notice the verbs that have been used to express the various actions.

> The circle of children closed around us, each child chanting, 'Fight! Fight! Fight!' until the sound rang in my ears and, hitting out blindly, I landed the first punch. Jo darted away, bellowing with rage. Recovering, he hurled himself at me until I lost my footing and crashed to the ground where I lay, winded and dazed. Above me a sea of faces peered down, some concerned, others distorted with fury. Jo threw himself on top of me and we continued struggling until, worn out and drained of anger, we were separated.

By using precise verbs you can describe movements exactly and produce a colourful and accurate piece of writing.

For you to do

Using words from the passage above and those listed below to help you, write a short account of a boxing or wrestling match. As well as describing the actions of the fighters, refer to the crowd, the noise and the fervent atmosphere.

punch	dash	dodge
lurch	swing	bawl
bound	scuffle	fervid
hurl	roar	heated
swerve	thrilling	combative
evade	stirred	frenzied
scream	belligerent	unrest
impassioned	clash	target
controversy	wrangle	exhausted
brawl	spring	sway
resist	drag	

Checkpoints

- Concentrate on expressing your ideas exactly and vividly.
- You will find that it takes time to choose the precise words that exactly convey your ideas, but as you extend your vocabulary the search for the right word will become easier.
- Succinct and expressive vocabulary can improve spoken and written accounts and descriptions.

Chapter 22 Being Formal

What does 'being formal' involve?

It involves being able to:
- identify formal situations
- distinguish between informal and formal vocabulary
- choose the correct formal vocabulary and style suitable for your audience, situation and to create a formal tone.

Why is it important to be formal?

- Certain situations and audiences require a formal style.
- Using informal language in the wrong situations can let you down.
- You can lose marks in some exams and in your coursework if you make the wrong choice.
- This chapter:
  - considers when to use formal language
  - gives you words and phrases that are suitable for formal situations
  - shows you how the words you choose affect the formality of your message.

Formal language

- Formal language shouldn't be stilted and unnatural, full of long words and complicated sentences.
- It should be exact, effective and suit your purpose and audience.
- Always consider:

  What is my purpose?
  What do I want to achieve?
  What is the best way of achieving this?

  Who is my audience?
  Am I familiar with them?
  What will they expect from me?
  What might influence them?

  What is the appropriate tone to use?
  Should I be formal or informal?
  Should I be: firm, persuasive, informative, conciliatory, etc?

■ When you have considered the answers to these questions, you can begin to choose appropriate vocabulary for the task.

Common mistakes

What impression do you gain of the firm and divisional manager from this letter? Is the style and vocabulary appropriate for a letter to a customer?

Craven Supplies
Unit 1a
Piddinghoe Industrial Estate
East Sussex
BN4 3EB
Tel: 01273 697879

October 9th 19—

Mrs E. Flaherty
Bilston Chemicals
Reeve Lane
Chichester
West Sussex
PO4 7TY

Order Reference Number: BH23/897P

Dear Mrs Flaherty

Thanks for your letter. We got it yesterday. Our new girl's dealing with it and you'll get it soon. You know us – good service and prompt delivery.

Don't forget, as usual, any problems or anything I can do for you, Pete's the name, just give us a bell.

As ever

Pete Lomas

Pete Lomas
Divisional Manager

■ This is a formal work situation and Mr Lomas is providing a customer with information. He probably doesn't know the customer personally. A formal style and vocabulary are needed.

Now read this transcript of a recorded message left on an Inland Revenue Department's answering machine.

> Bill Smithie here. I'd like the girl I had a natter with yesterday to give me a ring tomorrow. Don't know her name but she sounded a bit like my sister. Tell her I want a bit of info about Schedule D as I'm getting in a right muddle. I need an expert pronto. I'm sure she'll remember my number but here it is all the same – 567832.

▧ The woman dealing with Mr Smithie's tax affair may well object to his informal, chatty, over-familiar style. She may feel less inclined to ring him promptly and offer her help. She may even feel that his accounts need very careful scrutiny!

▧ In both examples the writer and caller have used chatty, informal language unsuited to the situation and failed to consider their audiences, the tone of their messages or the degree of formality required. Their messages have lost their impact and effectiveness because of their misjudgement.

Formal writing tasks

▧ A formal writing style is appropriate for the following tasks:
  ▶ essays
  ▶ letters
  ▶ reports
  ▶ promotional leaflets
  ▶ instructions
  ▶ at work – memos.

Essays
▧ In an essay you may need to:
  ▶ be descriptive
  ▶ be imaginative
  ▶ be informative
  ▶ outline a process or event
  ▶ argue a point of view.
▧ An essay is often the supreme test of your writing skills, and must:
  ▶ be well-planned
  ▶ have a logical order
  ▶ fully answer the question
  ▶ be relevant

- contain well-chosen, precise, formal vocabulary
- contain a wide variety of appropriate words and phrases.
- You should avoid the use of:
  - colloquial words and phrases (see Chapter 19)
  - clichés (see Chapter 18)
  - tautology (see Chapter 18)
  - verbosity (see Chapter 18).
- In essays written for GCSE English, examiners are looking for evidence of a wide vocabulary to express meanings with clarity and precision.

Formal letters

These are extracts from formal letters.

> The results of the recent Monitoring Progress Exercise for your division are listed below. Please refer to the sheet attached which is provided to help you in understanding the implications for your division.

> A new barrier will be erected at the East Wing Car Park on Friday November 23rd. All staff will be issued with a key which can be obtained from the Head of Administration in room A214 between 1 pm and 2 pm on November 21st and 22nd. A deposit of £5 must be paid for each key.

- Every letter has a job to do. A formal letter should be brief, polite, clear, accurate and informative. The words you choose are important: they affect the tone of your letter.
- The same words and phrases keep appearing in formal letters.

Examples: I would be grateful if you could …
I wish to apply for the position of …
I would be grateful if you could provide me with information about …
Please do not hesitate to contact me if you require any further information …
Thank you for your letter which I received on …
I am sorry that you found cause to complain about …
The advertisement stated …

- Obviously, the examples here are very general; the choice of words you need depends on the situation and purpose of your letter.
- When you receive formal letters, note down words and phrases which could be useful to you when you write formal letters.

Formal speaking situations

■ You may need to speak in a formal style in these situations:
  ▶ interviews
  ▶ inputs at meetings
  ▶ votes of thanks
  ▶ discussions
  ▶ instructions.

Look back at page 83. Mr Smithie's answerphone message would have been more effective if he had said something like this:

> This is Bill Smithie. My telephone number is 567832. I would be grateful if the officer I spoke to yesterday could telephone me tomorrow to give me some information about Schedule D.

Advice

■ Whenever possible, plan what you are going to say before you begin.

■ In formal speaking tasks you should aim to be brief, clear and polite.

■ Omit irrelevant details and concentrate on getting your message across as precisely and accurately as possible.

■ Don't try to impress your audience by using complicated words and phrases. The best English is simple and direct; the worst is verbose and obscure.

■ In GCSE English your teachers and the examiners are looking at your ability to use the vocabulary and grammar of standard English; express yourself clearly; adapt your speech to the situation; and listen, understand and respond appropriately to others. A wide vocabulary and the ability to distinguish formal from informal language will help you achieve these goals.

Checkpoints

■ Be aware of what constitutes a formal situation.

■ Remember, the words you use affect the formality of a situation.

■ Use precise, formal vocabulary.

■ Express yourself briefly, clearly, politely and with confidence.

Glossary

Antonyms	Words that have the opposite meaning to each other (compare **synonyms**).
Cliché	Hackneyed expression.
Colloquial language	Conversational or everyday words.
Compound word	A word made up of two or more individual words, e.g. blackberries (black + berries)
Consonant	A letter of the alphabet *other than* **a**, **e**, **i**, **o** or **u** (compare *vowel*). The letter **y** can be described as half vowel and half consonant: in words like **why** and **dry** it sounds like the vowel **i**, but in words like **yawn** and **yard** it has a consonant sound.
Homophone	A word that sounds the same as another but has a different spelling and meaning.
Noun	A naming word: a noun can be the name of a thing, person, place, animal, quality, emotion or idea.
Plural	More than one person or item (compare *singular*).
Prefix	A group of letters added to the beginning of a *root word* to alter the meaning of the word, e.g. **dis**satisfied **un**known **il**legal
Root word	A word, complete in itself, which can have a *prefix* or *suffix* added to it, e.g. re cover ing prefix root word suffix
Syllable	A word or part of a word that can be made by one effort of breath, e.g. drink *one syllable* paper *two syllables* pa / per refreshment *three syllables* re / fresh / ment A syllable always contains a **vowel** or a **y**.
Singular	One person or item (compare *plural*).
Suffix	A group of letters added to the end of a *root word*, e.g. walk**ing** treat**ment**
Consonant suffix	A suffix that begins with a *consonant*, e.g. lone**ly** hard**ship**
Vowel suffix	A suffix that begins with a *vowel*, e.g. skat**ing** laugh**able**

86

Synonyms	Words that have a similar meaning to each other (compare *antonyms*).
Tautology	Unnecessarily repeating the same idea in different words.
Verb	A word of action.
Verbosity	Using a large number of words or complicated words and phrases to express an idea.
Vowel	Any of the letters **a, e, i, o** or **u** (compare *consonant*).
Short vowel	A vowel that makes a short sound, e.g. **a** in mad **e** in ten **i** in window **o** in lost **u** in humble
Long vowel	A single vowel that makes a long sound (the same sound as its name), e.g. **a** in mate **e** in compete **i** in fine **o** in clothe **u** in cube